cu

st

cultural studies

Will Brooker

TEACH YOURSELF BOOKS

For UK order queries: please contact Bookpoint Ltd, 39 Milton Park, Abingdon, Oxon OX14 4TD. Telephone: (44) 01235 400414, Fax: (44) 01235 400454. Lines are open from 9.00–6.00, Monday to Saturday, with a 24-hour message answering service. Email address: orders@bookpoint.co.uk

For U.S.A. & Canada order queries: please contact NTC/Contemporary Publishing, 4255 West Touhy Avenue, Lincolnwood, Illinois 60646–1975, U.S.A. Telephone: (847) 679 5500, Fax: (847) 679 2494.

Long-renowned as the authoritative source for self-guided learning – with more than 30 million copies sold worldwide – the *Teach Yourself* series includes over 200 titles in the fields of languages, crafts, hobbies, sports, and other leisure activities.

British Library Cataloguing in Publication Data
A catalogue entry for this title is available from The British Library

Library of Congress Catalog Card Number: On file

First published in UK 1998 by Hodder Headline Plc, 338 Euston Road, London NW1 3BH

First published in US 1999 by NTC/Contemporary Publishing, 4255 West Touhy Avenue, Lincolnwood (Chicago), Illinois 60646–1975, U.S.A.

Typeset by Transet Limited, Coventry, England.
Printed in Great Britain for Hodder & Stoughton Educational, a division of Hodder Headline Plc, 338 Euston Road, London NW1 3BH by Cox & Wyman Ltd, Reading, Berkshire.

Impression number	10 9 8 7 6 5 4 3 2
Year	2002 2001 2000 1999

Thanks to Liz, Pete and Joe, who continue to teach me.

CONTENTS

Introduction _____ **1**
Why Cultural Studies? _____ 1
About this book _____ 2
Further reading _____ 5

1 | Precursors and Precedents _____ **6**
Anarchy in the UK: Matthew Arnold _____ 6
The old and the new: F.R. Leavis _____ 11
Resisting the culture industry: T.W. Adorno _____ 16

2 | Founding Fathers _____ **23**
Look back in nostalgia: Richard Hoggart _____ 23
A feeling for change: Raymond Williams _____ 31

3 | Ideologies of the Everyday _____ **41**
Roland Barthes _____ 42
John Berger _____ 48

4 | Birmingham and Beyond _____ **59**
Origins: Stuart Hall and the CCCS _____ 59
Styles of resistance: Dick Hebdige _____ 64
Negotiating the television audience: David Morley___ 70
Invisible girls: Angela McRobbie _____ 75

5 | The French Connection _____ **82**
Structures of power: Michel Foucault _____ 83
Structures of taste: Pierre Bourdieu _____ 89
Living in the gaps: Michel de Certeau _____ 94

6 | States of Reception _____ **101**
Negotiating the popular: John Fiske _____ 101
Feminism and the romance: Janice Radway _____ 108
Powers of fandom: Henry Jenkins _____ 113

7 | Doing Cultural Studies _____ **122**
Hartleyism _____ 122

8 | Where Next? _____ **131**

Further Reading _____ **140**

Useful Addresses _____ **141**

Index _____ **142**

INTRODUCTION

Why Cultural Studies?

> What are now called departments of English will be renamed
> departments of 'Cultural Studies' where Batman comics, Mormon
> theme parks, television, movies and rock will replace Chaucer,
> Shakespeare, Milton, Wordsworth and Wallace Stevens.
>
> Harold Bloom, *The Western Canon*

Cultural Studies, as Harold Bloom's doomy pronouncement suggests, has
not yet gained an aura of academic 'respectability'. It has become a
common sneer, and an easy one, to deride 'Cult Studs' as an extension of the
'trendy teaching' which is said to be replacing traditional methods in
education.

Obviously, I take Cultural Studies seriously – as you indicate you're
prepared to, even by coming this far – and I hope to show in this book,
among other things, that the subject has a fairly long and indisputably
distinguished heritage. Yet I think there is something to value in the
continuing marginality, even the radicalism associated with the subject; in
the fact that Cultural Studies is not entirely approved of, not fully
assimilated into the academy. It suggests that this is still a subject very
much alive with a healthy kick, still with a certain edge and therefore still
able to carry out the jobs it was meant for: that is, engaging with the living
detail of the everyday, the popular and sometimes the underside of
culture. This kind of culture is always fluid and vibrant because it is
always being formed and reshaped in relationship with those who
encounter, consume and interact with it and these audiences – though we
could call them 'readers' or even co-creators – are also the 'subjects' of
Cultural Studies.

Cultural Studies, as sketched by my inevitably limited discussion in this
book, has drawn within its boundaries studies of 1930s jazz and 1970s

punk, the milk bars of the 1950s and the amusement arcades of the 1980s, advertisements from the beginning, middle and end of this century and pulp fiction from dime novels to Mills and Boon romances to *Jackie* photostories – and yes, even Batman comics might get a look in. Like Bloom, you may look at this list and conclude that these are trivial ephemera, unworthy of academic study, testament to the decline of contemporary education. In which case we should probably part company now. Alternatively, you may pick the 'right' answer and open the box that is Cultural Studies and I will assume you share my view that these are vital signs of how we construct our culture and how that culture constructs us; points of interaction between text and reader and producer and back again, through which each one shapes and defines the other. If so, as those trendy teachers might say, join the trip.

If you're with Bloom but still hanging on this far, do remember at least that these judgements of taste and quality, as many writers I discuss in this book fluently demonstrate, are not fixed standards but temporary constructs of a particular period. The theorists we now regard as pioneers and founding fathers of Cultural Studies would indeed have shared some of Bloom's distaste for the products of 'mass culture', although they differed from him in thinking those products worthy of study if only to educate their readers against them; as the discipline evolved, notions of 'good' and 'bad' culture were shown to be fluid and dependent on a particular social project or political climate. It has become a truism that Shakespeare and Dickens, in their own times, were no less 'popular', no more a part of 'high' culture than the comic book is today; a truism that must need repeating, for some commentators are evidently incapable of applying its lesson to our contemporary texts. For what it's worth, the most popular forms of the 1980s and 1990s may well become part of the respected academic canon of the twenty-first century; so why wait? Get them while they're still warm.

About this book

It would be possible, as demonstrated by several other books which I recommend at the end of this section, to introduce the field of Cultural Studies by splitting it into 'concepts'. We might have a section on 'Audience' followed by chapters on 'The Popular', on 'Gender', even 'Hegemony'. This is not the approach I have chosen.

My reasons are twofold. Firstly, I feel that this approach has the disadvantage of collecting theories or case studies produced at very different cultural and historical moments under one catch-all banner, and runs the risk of glossing over those important differences for the sake of a structural convenience. For the reader new to the subject, I can't help feeling that such 'concepts' may seem unhelpfully abstract, like balloons too large to grasp. I am attempting, instead, to weight down those concepts by taking 'Cultural Studies' at its most literal, as 'studies of culture': studies carried out in specific social, academic and national contexts, with specific aims and agenda, at specific times.

I am taking what may seem the rather traditional step of placing these studies in chronological order, while allowing for a number of significant overlaps. Cultural Studies did not come into being all at once. It developed and evolved, through a succession of individuals and groups who were not always aware of and certainly not always in agreement with each other's work, and there is a story to be told from it. Many of the writers discussed in this book were aware of their position in that story, and were glad to acknowledge their debt to those who had gone before: certainly today I think there are few people in Cultural Studies who are not conscious and often proud of the heritage which informs their own work and which their own work in turn continues.

It's in this spirit of a continuing heritage that I can turn to Raymond Williams to justify my choice of approach, although I may have qualms about drawing my modest project here into any kind of parallel with his great work *Culture and Society*. Williams is seeking to explore 'key words', like the two in his title; not, as the first method I suggested above would, through 'a series of abstracted problems', but through 'a series of statements by individuals'.

> I have not chosen to list certain topics, and to assemble summaries of particular statements on them. I have, rather, with only occasional exceptions, concentrated on particular thinkers and their actual statements, and tried to understand and value them. The framework of the enquiry is general, but the method, in detail, is the study of actual individual statements and contributions.
>
> Raymond Williams, *Culture and Society 1780–1950*, p.xix

This book, then, is split into six main chapters taking Cultural Studies from what I, because the starting line has to be drawn somewhere, consider its prehistory, to a sampling of the most recent developments in the field. Towards the end is an interview with John Hartley, author of *Popular Reality* (1996) and *Uses of Television* (1999), and editor of the *International Journal of Cultural Studies*, which was launched in 1998. Among other things this penultimate chapter offers an insight, by no means representative but I believe unique and useful, into the actual research processes behind a recent work of cultural theory.

Each chapter, like that last, is structured around case studies of key writers from a specific cultural and historical moment. This approach, as I have suggested, enables a close discussion of individual texts in some detail, from which conceptual issues readily emerge. It also has the side-effect of inviting argument about the selection of 'key writers'. About the majority of these I feel there can be very little dispute and I discuss their work because I feel they are widely acknowledged as major contributors to the field. Inevitably though, once the 'greats' are dispensed with and we begin to focus on more recent work, everyone will have their own preferences; and I have chosen mine sometimes on the grounds of the accessibility and relevance of their work to the reader unfamiliar with this discipline, partly because they represent a key strand in Cultural Studies without which I feel any overview would be incomplete and, overall, unavoidably, for purely subjective reasons. Many of the writers discussed here have given me pleasure as well as 'work' and I hope I can communicate some of that in turn.

Each section on an individual writer begins with an introduction, placing them in a context and a relation to those discussed previously. Cultural Studies, like culture itself, is a process and a dialogue, so after each survey of a key text I raise problems with that text and its writer and ask questions of both. These are partly questions and problems raised by others within the 'tradition', either contemporary or following afterwards, and partly my own: and my point is, put simply, to encourage you to ask your own questions of them. Cultural Studies is not yet a fossilised canon of indisputable 'truths'. If it is not to become fossilised, it must remain in debate; and there's no reason you can't challenge someone just because they were published in the 1940s.

Finally, each section ends with not just a bibliography of work by the author in question, but a series of links within this book and some more diverse suggestions for further reading around the subject. There is a lot of value in the motto 'only connect': it is through making links, comparisons and parallels that these texts remain in dialogue with each other, and being able to draw those connecting lines yourself is as rewarding a way as any to feel you are beginning to engage with Cultural Studies. This book itself is part of that network of discourse; it is a minor connecting point. I will be frank: you cannot 'teach yourself' Cultural Studies through this book, if that implies that when you reach the last page you will be taught and you will have finished. You will never be finished. What you can do through this book is make a start. You can begin to teach yourself Cultural Studies with this book, if you treat it as the minor connecting point it is and trace its routes back to the original texts and beyond them to the further reading and beyond them to other texts which you suddenly realise have another connection. You will have started, and by then perhaps you won't ever want to finish.

Further reading

During, Simon, *The Cultural Studies Reader*, Routledge, 1993

Storey, John, *What Is Cultural Studies: A Reader*, Arnold, 1996

Storey, John, *Cultural Theory and Popular Culture: An Introduction*, Harvester Wheatsheaf, 1997

Strinati, Dominic, *An Introduction to Theories of Popular Culture*, Routledge, 1995

Turner, Graeme, *British Cultural Studies: An Introduction*, Routledge, 1990

1 | PRECURSORS AND PRECEDENTS

Anarchy in the UK: Matthew Arnold

Why Matthew Arnold? Any attempt to choose a starting point for the birth of a discipline or area of study is destined to be contentious. Some would trace Cultural Studies back another stop to Samuel Taylor Coleridge; others would rather begin later, with F.R. Leavis. I choose Arnold because this point of origin, arbitrary as it may be, gives a sense of the 'great tradition' which shadows contemporary work on culture and which lends the discipline as a whole a richness and depth; Arnold was writing a full century before the Birmingham School began to investigate Britain in the 1960s and yet his criticism retains enough relevance and immediacy to offer a counterpoint to those more recent enquiries. Secondly, the work for which Arnold is most celebrated after *Culture and Anarchy* – essays on literature, the function of the critic and poetic theory and, to a lesser extent, his own poetry – demonstrates the links, at this early stage of its evolution, between Cultural Studies and literary criticism. Some might dismiss Arnold's work as too sweeping and generalised to be classed as Cultural Studies as we now understand the term, rather than social criticism: I would counter that *Culture and Anarchy* supports its arguments with reference to specific readings in London's House of Commons, exact transcriptions from the editorials of *The Times* newspaper and quotations from named critics, and so draws as much on the everyday culture surrounding Arnold as the work of contemporary writers pulls its examples from MTV, tabloid journalism and advertisement hoardings.

Arnold was born in 1822, the son of a headmaster and educational reformer. He won prizes for poetry at Rugby and Oxford then, at the age of 25, became the personal secretary to Lord Lansdowne, a Whig politician in a post equivalent, in the current British system, to Minister for Education. In 1851 he accepted from Lansdowne the position of

Inspector of Schools and, as such, travelled across England and Europe, investigating mainly the severe Protestant establishments known as Nonconformist, or Dissenting schools; his work in France, Holland and Switzerland resulted in the essay 'Democracy' of 1861 and, more generally, his views of Dissenters – or Puritans as he sometimes called them – fed into *Culture and Anarchy*. Meanwhile Arnold had been elected Professor of Poetry at Oxford, England, in 1857, a post which required him to produce three lectures a year and helped to secure his position as the foremost literary critic of the period. He retired in 1886 and died two years later.

Culture and Anarchy (1867–9)

That lack of a single date alone suggests that Arnold's key work of social criticism was not written and published in the way we currently expect. The first chapter appeared in 1867 and the remainder followed periodically until this series of articles could be bound as a whole and subtitled as 'an essay' in 1869. This process results in the phenomenon of Arnold responding in his third chapter to critics of the first; it is a striking feature and I think a positive one, as it makes the book a true dialogue, a work of argument, polemic and often satire. Arnold's manner, while not perhaps conversational, does suggest a spoken delivery, with all the rhetorical device and snide point-scoring of a good parliamentary speech; once you slip into his rhythms he can be genuinely funny.

Arnold's main thesis here is pretty well contained in the title: Society is heading towards Anarchy, and only Culture can save it. Culture, as Arnold sees it, is painted in rosy tones in the first chapter, 'Sweetness and Light'. The threat of anarchy stems from the contemporary philosophy of 'Doing as one Likes', which happens to be the title of the second chapter. Straightforward enough.

'Doing as one Likes' was to Arnold in danger of becoming the dominant impulse of the period, spreading outwards from the Liberal Party which in turn was home of the Dissenters or Nonconformists and so stood for much that Arnold opposed – while paradoxically 'liberal' in many ways himself, Arnold distanced himself from the political party by titling himself 'a Liberal of the future'. In one of the principal metaphors of the book, this impulse is described as 'Hebraist' – that is, in the spirit of the Hebrew – as opposed to 'Hellenist', the Greek project of perfection in all spheres, which Arnold places on the side of 'Culture'. So the game-plan of *Culture and Anarchy* begins to take shape: Culture, Sweetness and Light and

Hellenism are Good Things, while Anarchy, Doing as one Likes and Hebraism are the opposition.

Hebraism and Hellenism

Arnold wheels this model in midway through *Culture and Anarchy*; but as it becomes an overarching frame for the whole book, it is best explained first.

Arnold posits that society, throughout history, has been governed by two forces: one is an energy towards duty, self-control and work, and the other towards knowledge and ideas. He names them after the two races he sees as best embodying these impulses – the Hebrews and the Greeks. Hebraism sees its purpose in 'firm obedience' and 'strictness of conscience', and Hellenism in 'clear intelligence', 'thinking clearly', 'spontaneity of consciousness'. Christianity was a triumph of Hebraism and the Renaissance – or 'Renascence' as Arnold calls it – a glory of Hellenism; so the two alternate throughout history until Arnold's Victorian England, after the Protestant Reformation and its return to the Bible, sees Hebraism with the upper hand.

Hebraism isn't a bad thing in itself. Indeed, the two impulses are not presented as dramatically opposed by nature – Arnold spends pages spelling out their similarities in terms of a final aim in salvation or perfection and finding echoes of one in the other – but have become rivals through their use throughout history. Arnold sees much value in Hebraism, but believes that now is the wrong time for it to be in the ascendant. The rise of Puritanism in the sixteenth century checked the progress of Hellenism, as embodied by the Renaissance, so contemporary society is governed by an impulse of conscience and control when it could far better be guided by the Hellenist project of seeing things clearly and seeking knowledge. Arnold only warns against Hebraism because its dominance put a stop to the advances of Hellenism; ideally, he would see both in balance and sees it as his job to bring something of Hellenism to bear against the Dissenters of his period.

Doing as one likes

Arnold's targets are Liberalism and Puritanism; and in this combination alone there is a seeming contradiction. How does Hebraism, the doctrine of duty and obedience, tally with the idea of doing what one likes? The answer is that duty, in the eyes of Arnold's opponents, is only to the letter of the law – in this case, the Bible – beyond which an individual retains his treasured liberty. Arnold gives an excellent example in his discussion of a case in London's House of Commons, when Thomas Chambers, MP for Marylebone, brought forward his bill for enabling a man to marry his deceased wife's sister.

> His first point was that God's law, – the name he always gave to the Book of Leviticus, – did not really forbid a man to marry his deceased wife's sister. God's law not forbidding it, the Liberal maxim, that a man's prime right and happiness is to do as he likes, ought at once to come into force, and to annul any such check on the assertion of personal liberty as the prohibition to marry one's deceased wife's sister.
>
> (1891 edition, p.139)

That is, if you're not specifically prohibited from doing something, it must follow that you're allowed to do it. We can see that duty and obedience to 'God's law', as interpreted by the Liberals, paradoxically acted as *carte blanche* to the notion of doing as one liked.

Barbarians, Philistines, Populace and Aliens

The first three terms, adopted as a shorthand for the upper, middle and lower classes, have become one of Arnold's most enduring legacies. Each group, he says, despite their social differences, value above all else the liberty to do as they like; yet the activities they pursue in their happy liberty vary from field-sports for the Barbarian through the Philistine's 'tea-meetings' down to the Populace's 'beer'. Each class has a darker side, though, and while Arnold attributes to the Barbarian and Philistine the harmless pleasures of honours and business, the Populace is accused of liking 'bawling, hustling and smashing'. This phrase is a nod towards the single event which reverberates throughout the book, acting as a symbol of Anarchy: the Hyde Park riots of July 1866, during which a crowd pulled down the iron railings surrounding the park. Compared to this act of physical rowdyism, the Philistine liberty enshrined in misguided Acts of Parliament seems fairly harmless and it is hard not to conclude that the anarchy Arnold most fears is embodied by the Populace: a fear of the 'mass' and a working class without any curbs to stop it doing as it likes.

Where, then, should salvation come from? From 'aliens'. As Arnold uses the word, he means individuals from whatever class who do not fit in with the dominant spirit of that class, and instead are motivated by a 'humane spirit, by the love of human perfection'; this is the army Arnold wants to recruit in the pursuit of Culture. In opposition to his critics, who see

Culture as something trivial, silly and pedantic, to Arnold Culture is the study of perfection, the impulse to do good and to make the world good; an expansion over and above individual achievement, or gain for the sake of itself, or greatness in one specific area, and in keeping with the holistic impulse of the Greeks he so admires, whose efforts were all geared towards 'some ideal of complete human perfection and happiness.' And if that sounds vague, so it was. It was made slightly more specific by Arnold's claim that Culture was preserved in the canon of great literature and poetry. Cultural attainment could therefore be measured with reference to the ideals promoted within key literary touchstones and, conveniently for Arnold, the literary critic was correspondingly elevated through this process to the role of cultural examiner.

Problems with Arnold

Arnold's project to lift 'Culture' out of the sphere of the trivial and ineffectual and into a far wider role as a vital part in any struggle to improve society is a valuable one, with lasting implications. However, all his recommendations remain supremely vague and abstract, and he makes no practical suggestions as to how the genuine problems of poverty and overcrowding which he sympathetically describes should be improved. We might also question his advocacy of a sovereign State, on the grounds that 'without order there can be no society, and without society there can be no human perfection'; to work for Culture through articles and dialogue is one thing, to administer it from on high is another, particularly when Arnold's conception of 'sweetness and light' is put forward in such a narrow and selective form. Finally, although he stresses that the elements of Barbarian, Philistine and Populace are present within us all, Arnold's famous demarcations tend to reinforce a sense of class divisions which rather than being fluid or open to change operate as eternal categories like 'Hellenistic'. Raymond Williams, several decades later, would have something to say on the negative effects of these divisions, and on the pathological fear of the 'mass' from which Arnold trembles, almost, it seems, despite his best intentions.

Further reading

The Complete Prose Works of Matthew Arnold (ed. R.H. Super, 11 vols, Ann Arbor, 1960–77)

Matthew Arnold: Selected Works (ed. Miriam Allott, R.H. Super, Oxford, 1986)

There are many books on Arnold and his work; a useful first choice, and one of the most recent, is Stefan Collini's *Arnold* (Oxford University Press, 1988). You might want to look at some of Arnold's poetry which, like *Culture and Anarchy*, often draws on a romantic portrait of the Greeks as counterpoint to a contemporary situation; 'Dover Beach', one of his most famous, is an example. *The Poems of Matthew Arnold* (ed. Kenneth Allott, London, 1979) is a standard edition.

Links in this book

Raymond Williams can usefully be brought to bear on Arnold; *Culture and Society* deals specifically with him and *The Long Revolution* raises the more general issues alluded to above. My heading 'Anarchy in the UK' is not entirely facetious; I think it might be profitable to compare Arnold's visions of anarchy with the way it happened over a century later, on however small a scale, through Dick Hebdige's discussion of the Punk movement. Equally appropriate is Hebdige's account of other disruptive subcultures, whether Mod or Rasta, which evoked similar fears of the 'mob'. Stuart Hall's description of the attempts to contain another social group apparently doing as it liked, the 'black youth' of the 1970s, also casts an interesting light on Arnold's idealised vision of the authoritarian State.

The old and the new: F.R. Leavis

F.R. Leavis is best known for *The Great Tradition* (1948), whose subtitle *George Eliot, Henry James, Joseph Conrad* indicates something of its Top Ten approach to literary heritage. In our tour through the chronology of cultural studies, Leavis' most famous work offers few rewards: rather the landmark is the slim and often overlooked *Culture and Environment* of 1933, written by Leavis in collaboration with his colleague and former student Denys Thompson.

Leavis takes up the torch from Arnold in two related ways. He devoted himself to the rigorous study of literature and the shaping of this study into a critical academic discipline, and in turn he regarded literature – by which he meant a highly selective canon of 'great works' – as a treasure-house of aesthetic and moral values which offered salvation from a perceived decline in the standards of contemporary society. Like Arnold, Leavis saw 'society' as very much different from 'culture', the first signifying the cheap tawdriness of modern life and the latter a separate sphere, a kind of Mount Olympus where Shakespeare, Dante and some select others – Jane Austen and George Eliot, for instance, but not James Joyce or Virgina Woolf – gloried as examples of human achievement. Significantly, this 'modern life is rubbish' mentality, with its division between 'bad' society and an idealised, subjective 'culture' will continue, albeit with a refraction through the filter of Marxism, into the work of T.W. Adorno and his colleagues.

Frank Raymond Leavis was born on 14 July 1895. Following service as a medical orderly in the First World War he returned, in 1919, to his childhood home of Cambridge, England, where his father ran a bicycle shop. He took a degree in English and in 1924 completed his doctoral thesis on 'The relationship of journalism to literature: studied in the rise and earlier development of the press in England', whose slightly inelegant title already prefigured the issues Leavis would take up in *Culture and Environment*.

He began teaching at Cambridge in 1927. Two years later he married one of his students, who rejoiced in the name Queenie Dorothy and as Q.D. Leavis became Frank Raymond's longest-standing collaborator and a noted critic in her own right. One of Leavis' first published works, the pamphlet *Mass Civilisation and Minority Culture* of 1930, drew heavily on his wife's research thesis, which itself later appeared as *Fiction and the Reading Public*. In 1932 Leavis was appointed Director of Studies in English at Downing College, where he would remain for the next thirty years, and joined – with his wife and Denys Thompson – the editorial board of the new literary journal *Scrutiny*, for which he would write some of his best-known articles and shape his own influential vision of the critical literary canon. F.R. Leavis died in 1978.

Culture and Environment (1933)

Culture and Environment could almost be subtitled *Teach Yourself Cultural Studies*. The book's project is one of benevolent education; it is a guidebook for teachers and students, for classwork and self-teaching, with a postscript comprising a list of exercises and essay topics. Its aim is to teach a critical awareness of the texts and artefacts of contemporary culture, much as an undergraduate course in Media might do today. Indeed, many of Leavis' exercises could be lifted directly from this 1933 volume to a modern seminar room without much modification: the suggestions for close analysis of British newspapers – the *Manchester Guardian* contrasted with the *Mail*, *The Times* and the *Express* – are dated only by the the *Guardian's* defunct former title, while undergraduates are still tackling essays today on another of Leavis' topics, 'The History of the Newspaper-Press during the last half-century'. Leavis' pedagogic approach enjoys the occasional light touch – readers are asked to wonder 'what a Martian would think of our civilisation if he had only a copy of a penny-newspaper to judge by' – and is admirably cross-curricular, drawing in history, literary criticism and even science, when he mordantly suggests that students try to determine 'the amount of palm and olive oils in Palmolive Soap'. The project becomes increasingly self-reflexive as Leavis quotes from his own pamphlets, recommends *Scrutiny* without a murmur of his own involvement and in turn encourages the student-reader to examine his or her own essays for examples of literary skill. All in all, Leavis is an imaginative teacher, combining a wide range of secondary references from Arnold to D.H. Lawrence with a savvy of primary texts such as pulp novels and advertising copy.

Unlike most teachers of cultural studies today, though, Leavis despises this flotsam of modern culture; his aim is to teach a greater awareness of journalism, advertising and popular fiction solely in order that the reader can more shrewdly see through the workings of this tawdry culture and ultimately resist it.

High culture

Leavis' critical training is intended, then, to sharpen the reader's observation, awareness and powers of discrimination until he or she can see things as they really are. If this chimes with Arnold's 'Hellenism' the impression is supported by Leavis' heavy hints as to the culture he does approve of, as in the following parenthetical suggestion: '... classes moderately advanced in training might be asked to consider the probable concomitants of a change from the Bible, the Prayer-Book, Bunyan, Shakespeare and Milton as the main influences upon our emotional vocabulary, to newspapers, advertisements, best-sellers and the cinema.'

No doubt Austen, James, Eliot and Conrad would be allowed onto the first list; we're back to Leavis' Great Tradition, which is effectively a more specific version of Arnold's cure-all, Culture. Unlike Arnold's, though, Leavis' tonic for society's ills comes in two bottles: great literature and a nostalgic, older and better way of life, which we might call 'folk culture' had Leavis not already named it.

Organic culture

Leavis recreates this vision of a pre-mechanised community through George Sturt's two documentary accounts *Change in the Village* and *The Wheelwright's Shop*, which he brings into contrast with the grotesque portrait of modern, commercialised American life given by another book, *Star-Dust in Hollywood*. The life afforded us by mass culture is to Leavis shallow and cheap: it reduces us spiritually and emotionally and, in his implication, it feminises, even infantilises an English lifestyle which was once organic and muscular. In the older culture there is no artificial division between 'work' and 'leisure', and no need for sordid entertainment to fill the spaces. The worker is a craftsman, actively engaged in his job, taking pride in a well-made piece of equipment and pleasure in his surroundings. It is a modern version of this 'art of living', this ordinary, everyday awareness and understanding which the older culture would have called 'lore', which Leavis is trying to foster through his exercises on advertising and the press; to counter the alienation of the modern workplace and the false education of 'mass culture', he wants to restore in the individual a keen, questioning instinct and with it the older workers' 'dignified notion of their place in the community'. You wonder, although he never mentions it, whether memories of his father's bicycle shop were somewhere at the heart of this plea for a stronger loving world.

Problems with Leavis

Firstly, Leavis' portrait of the 'organic' culture is romanticised to the point of myth. The idyll of this dignified, rich life is barely credible and at any rate seems to be drawn entirely from secondary sources rather than direct experience; in this respect it makes Richard Hoggart's account of his own working-class upbringing, often criticised for its rose-tinted nostalgia, seem grubbily realistic by comparison.

Leavis' exercises and tasks are, as I have noted, in many ways imaginative and well-intended; but they are also unbearably loaded with their author's snobbishness. A list of phrases including 'short-haired executive' and 'regular guy' is tailed with the question 'why do we wince at the mentality that uses this idiom?' and above this the exercise asks of the terms 'creative' and 'personality' the bullying question 'why do you feel embarrassed when you find yourself using these words in the advertising way?'

Rather than invite debate, Leavis shames the student-reader into agreement much as the advertisements he detests blackmail the consumer with the subtle threat of social inferiority. A pupil in Leavis' class who dared question this elitist and explicitly anti-American line would not, you feel, last long.

Further reading

Although *The Great Tradition* is symptomatic of Leavis' approach to 'culture' rather than a work of cultural studies itself, it is a useful supplement as an account of Leavis' favourite things, and essential to a fuller study of Leavis himself. Other texts of note include the collections of *Scrutiny* essays *For Continuity* (1933), *Determinations* (1934), *Revaluation* (1936) and *The Common Pursuit* (1952), and the early volume *New Bearings in English Poetry* (1932).

Leavis' concept of the literary canon was shaped partly by the critical work of the poet T.S. Eliot, whose *Selected Essays* are published in a standard edition by Faber and Faber: 'Tradition and the Individual Talent' is particularly influential. Q.D. Leavis' *Fiction and the Reading Public*, reprinted by Folcroft Library Editions of New York in 1974, is also sound follow-up reading to *Culture and Environment*. Of books on Leavis, Francis Mulhern's *The Moment of 'Scrutiny'* (New Left Books, 1979) is recognised as an outstanding work, while Denys Thompson's *The Leavises: Recollections and Impressions* (Cambridge University Press, 1984) takes a personal angle and is another source for the essay by Williams mentioned above. I have found Michael Boll's introduction, simply titled *F.R. Leavis* (Routledge, 1988) an invaluable resource.

As a sidenote, Joyce's *Ulysses*, with its many witty musings on the nature of early advertising, is a good antidote to Leavis and his great tradition.

Links in this book

I suggested above that Leavis continues the Arnoldian tradition – his own bibliography in *Culture and Environment* recommends *Culture and Anarchy* as 'an indispensable classic' – and that his approach is intriguingly reflected in the distorting mirror of Adorno's work, considered immediately below. The relationship between Leavis and the work of his own successors Richard Hoggart and Raymond Williams is particularly suggestive and will become apparent in the next section. Putting it very crudely Williams, like Leavis, harks back to an organic community, but is less damning of modern society, while Hoggart falls into accord with the Leavisite great divide of 'folk culture good, mass culture bad', again denigrating anything American in the latter category, yet places more stress on the female role in the earlier society.

More distantly, John Berger also aims to teach an awareness of the strategies in modern advertising, and John Hartley too works in the legacy of *Culture and Environment*'s critical approaches to journalism, although his embracing of 'feminised', suburbanised mass-market texts would no doubt horrify Leavis.

Finally, for a poignant, almost haunting glimpse of Leavis as he appeared to others, it is well worth seeking out Williams' short essay 'Seeing a Man Running' in his collection *What I Came To Say*, which brings Leavis the man very sharply to the mind's eye.

Resisting the culture industry: T.W. Adorno

The work of T.W. Adorno offers a fascinating example of the way Leavism might have developed in a parallel universe. Both writers despair at the superficial degradation of American 'mass' culture at around the same period, and both hold up good objects – chosen purely subjectively, but presented as absolutes – as alternatives.

Yet while Leavis clings to his literary canon for salvation, Adorno looks to the modernist *avant-garde* – precisely the kind of work Leavis would have turned away at the door – and while Leavis works in a benevolent, liberal elitist tradition a few stops down the line from Arnold, Adorno's project draws on a form of Marxism.

Theodor Wiesengrund Adorno was born in Frankfurt in 1903 to Jewish-Italian parents, a successful wine merchant and a professional singer; brought up primarily by his mother and aunt, he was taught piano at an early age and began to develop the critical engagement with music which would emerge in his later writing. In 1924 Adorno received his doctorate at the University of Frankfurt, where he met his lifelong collaborator Max Horkheimer and in the same period came into contact with Walter Benjamin, an academic eleven years older than Adorno who would become a major influence and intellectual sparring-partner. Adorno studied philosophy and music from 1925–6 in Vienna and wrote critical essays on music, often in debate with Benjamin, as the 1930s took him to Frankfurt, Berlin and, for a time, Oxford. The rise of the Nazis in Germany forced his flight to the USA in 1938.

The Frankfurt Institute For Social Research, often called simply The Frankfurt School, had been established in 1923 and was, during its long history, associated with a pantheon of intellectual figures including Walter Benjamin, Herbert Marcuse, Max Horkheimer – who led the School after 1931 – Adorno himself and later Adorno's own assistant, Jurgen Habermas. Adorno joined the School in 1938, by which time it had relocated to New York and, in 1944 published with Horkheimer his best-known work, *Dialectic of Enlightenment*.

In the late 1940s Adorno and Horkheimer re-established the Institute in Frankfurt. Adorno continued to publish until his death in1969.

The culture industry

Adorno coined the term 'culture industry' having decided 'mass culture' was not a harsh enough label; 'mass culture' might suggest a popular art, of the people, while the culture industry as Adorno saw it was about an imposition of culture from above. Adorno's work was partly a critique of 'enlightenment', that is the project of scientific and rational progress which he believed – with some justification in terms of the Nazi Germany he had recently fled – had become a nightmare of scientific and rational control.

> The total effect of the culture industry is one of anti-enlightenment in which ... enlightenment, that is the progressive technical domination, becomes mass deception and is turned into a means of fettering consciousness.

Adorno is known as a 'difficult' writer, but the above passage in 'Culture Industry Reconsidered' states his position clearly enough and he goes on to illustrate his complaint through abundant examples. The key feature of the culture industry's products is standardisation coupled with pseudo-individualisation. That is, films within Hollywood genres, such as the Western, are fundamentally the same but distinguished from each other through such superficial elements as the star, dramatic location and perhaps the gimmick of a plot twist. Similarly, the competition between the Chrysler and General Motors models is entirely illusory and manufactured, just as Warners films are basically no different from those of Metro Goldwyn Mayer. The consumer is fooled into thinking he or she is exercising a free choice through the culture industry's armoury of tricksy devices, designed to imply difference or individuality: 'the standardised jazz improvisation ... the film star whose hair curls over her eye to demonstrate her originality' (*Dialectic of Enlightenment*).

The consumer aspires in vain to success through the proxies of 'ordinary' models and singing stars who embody the culture industry's promise that anyone can 'make it'; rebellion and dissonance are incorporated into the product in small amounts and thus made safe, as in Orson Welles' 'departures from the norm [which] are regarded as calculated mutations'. Meanwhile the more challenging works of earlier art are 'adapted' and vulgarised by the composer 'jazzing up Mozart' or the studio which 'scrutinises a work by Balzac or Hugo' for its blockbuster potential.

I have been parroting Adorno here for the purpose of representing his views rather than because I see no holes in his argument, but it is hard not to recognise some aspects of this account which would apply equally well to the culture of the late 1990s if we replaced Adorno's references to singing stars, Welles and Balzac with the reassuringly 'ordinary' Spice Girls, token 'bad boys' singer Liam Gallagher and soccer player Paul Gascoigne, Baz Luhrmann's *Romeo and Juliet*, Gwynneth Paltrow in *Emma* and ultimately the British National Lottery, which surely epitomises Adorno's claim that 'the triumph of ... the culture industry is that consumers feel compelled to buy and use its products even though they see through them'.

Use value and commodity fetishisation

One result of the culture industry's machinations is that culture is no longer appreciated for its 'use value' but its 'exchange value'; that is, it doesn't matter how warm a coat keeps you but whether it's an agnes b or Donna Karan. In Adorno's example from 'On the Fetish Character', 'the consumer is really worshipping the money that he himself has paid for the ticket to the Toscanini concert'; he doesn't have to enjoy the music or even attend the concert, as his 'success' is inscribed in the fact that he could afford it. As such, Adorno draws on the Marxist theory of 'commodity fetishism', in which consumer products are valued solely in themselves – divorced from the labour which produced them – and social relations are dominated by 'things', or possessions. Adorno extends Marx's argument by focusing specifically on cultural commodities, such as the music concert, which in effect have no use value. A designer coat will keep you warm as well as earning you social prestige, but the ticket to an expensive concert is valuable only in terms of showing off.

Conversely, the penalty for being 'inferior' in this sense – not knowing which names to drop, which labels to flaunt, which books to have on the coffee table – is social exclusion or scorn. 'One simply "has to" have seen

Mrs Miniver', Adorno sneers in *Dialectic of Enlightenment*, at the risk of becoming 'a stranger among us'; again, we can pick our own late-1990s equivalent – say, *Friends*, *ER*, *This Life* – and see that Adorno's complaint still has a ring of truth. There seems a quite personal bitterness behind some of his comments on this alienating process; the passage of 'On the Fetish Character', for instance, where he describes the 'hostility and aversion' risked by anyone who questions this state of affairs 'even in conversation' has an air of genuine hurt to it.

So a mentality of collecting and hoarding the 'right' cultural commodities replaces genuine enjoyment, as 'the prestige seeker replaces the connoisseur'. Individuality is stifled, 'replaced by the effort to imitate', and 'freedom' reduced to the choice between near-identical products. The consumer's genuine needs are disguised by the false needs for this year's model, the 'unmissable' film, the must-have album of the year, which the culture industry creates and in turn smugly satisfies.

Good art

Like Leavis, Adorno champions his own favourite things as alternatives to the cultural decline around him. In this case great art is not George Eliot but a 'difficult', experimental aesthetic; as he states in *Dialectic of Enlightenment*, 'the great work of art has always achieved self-negation'. Rather than imitation and polish, 'the great artists were never those who embodied a wholly flawless and perfect style, but those who used style as a way of hardening themselves against the chaotic expression of suffering, as a negative truth'. Art, then, must be challenging, painful, ecstatic, open to failure and, in practice, this allows Schoenberg, Picasso, Dadaism and Expressionism into Adorno's club while shutting out any forms of 'popular' art and music.

Good bad art

Yet Adorno isn't quite as elitist as he is sometimes painted. In a much-quoted letter to Benjamin of 3 March 1936 he identifies high art like Schoenberg and mass-consumer products like the American film as 'torn halves of an integral freedom, to which, however, they do not add up'. Years later he would reiterate this model in 'Culture Industry Reconsidered':

> To the detriment of both [the culture industry] forces together the spheres of high and low art, separated for thousands of years. The seriousness of high art is destroyed in speculation about its efficacy;

the seriousness of the lower perishes with the civilisational constraints imposed on the rebellious resistance inherent within it ...

So Adorno finds the 'negation' he reveres in 'some revue films, and especially in the grotesque and the funnies ... in those features which bring it close to the circus, in the self-justifying and nonsensical skill of riders, acrobats and clowns' (*Dialectic of Enlightenment*). After so much pessimism and bitterness, it is a relief to hear Adorno admit his pleasure in the absurd and his admiration of Marx; that is, the Marx of *A Night At the Opera*, whose destruction of a piano in one comic scene Adorno describes in not-quite sparkling prose as 'a most estimable piece of refined entertainment'.

Problems with Adorno

Finding problems with Adorno these days really is like shooting fish in a barrel. Both John Docker in *Postmodernism and Popular Culture* (University of Cambridge, 1994) and Dominic Strinati in *An Introduction to Theories of Popular Culture* (Routledge, 1995) pull few punches in their exposure of Adorno's flaws. Not only does Adorno presume the consumer to be a 'cultural dope', mindlessly victim to the entertainment industry without any way of making his or her own individual use of the products, but he claims insight into the mental process of these individuals, describing with contempt dupes such as 'the girl whose satisfaction consists solely in the fact that she and her boyfriend "look good"'; there is no suggestion that these assertions are backed with audience research or indeed that Adorno would ever have lowered himself either to talk to these people or genuinely sample their culture himself. On the simplest level, Adorno is merely imposing his own precious tastes on a culture he doesn't and doesn't want to understand; any closer examination of the music or film industries of the time and certainly since would reveal a greater dissimilarity and dissonance than Adorno cares to admit.

The key factor in Adorno's defence remains his cultural position. He had escaped from Germany as it fell under an increasing state control of culture and found himself in the USA during a period of far greater cultural and industrial standardisation than today. Indeed, the warnings which burst repeatedly from Adorno's grim account – a comparison of the popular orchestral conductor with 'the totalitarian Fuehrer', the statement that 'the bourgeois ... is already virtually a Nazi' – indicate that he deeply feared the parallels with Nazi Germany which he saw emerging in the

United States. In this light his notorious pessimism is perhaps forgivable. He also takes care, contrary to some opinions, to illustrate his polemic with a variety of topical cultural references from Lana Turner to the Lone Ranger and even labours at one point to compare the culture industry's illusory 'freedom' with a saucy cartoon showing a girl eloping with her boyfriend, not realising that her father is holding the ladder beneath them. While he will never go down as one of the great populists, Adorno's flashes of humanity belie his stereotype as a sour elitist.

Further reading

Adorno's work is not always readily available in translation. Key works for completists include *Prisms* (1967) and his last major statements *Negative Dialectics* (1973) and *Aesthetic Theory* (1984) which was unfinished at his death and published posthumously. A collection of Adorno's essays, edited with a dense Introduction by J.M. Bernstein, is published as *The Culture Industry* (Routledge, 1991).

Books on Adorno and his colleagues include T. Bottomore's *The Frankfurt School* (Routledge, 1989) and Martin Jay's *The Dialectical Imagination* (Heinemann, 1973). The crucial text to a fuller understanding of Adorno, though, is Walter Benjamin's essay 'The Work of Art in the Age of Mechanical Reproduction'. First published in 1936, Benjamin's article can be seen as part of a polemical dialogue with Adorno's work of the period such as 'On The Fetish Character in Music' of 1938: *contra* Adorno, Benjamin argues that the mechanical reproduction of the artwork, shattering the quasi-mystical 'aura' which surrounds the original, is a positive step in that it makes the work available to a mass public, changing the sanctified status and ritualised viewing of art, and opens it to a new means of perception. The sound cinema and mass-produced photograph allow art to escape from private galleries and salons and permit the general public to enjoy, participate in and interact with art much as they would have done with the open and 'democratic' art forms of the great building or epic poem. The essay can be found collected in *Illuminations* (Fontana, 1973)

Links in this book

The connections with Leavis should by now be obvious and those with Hoggart and Williams will, I hope, become so. Adorno's comments on advertising, particularly on the Watney's poster in which a 'brand of beer was presented like a political slogan' ('On the Fetish Character') find an echo in John Berger's account decades later of the same phenomenon – 'publicity can translate even revolution into its own terms', he notes, over a poster for 'REVOLUTIONAIRY – the Perfect Panti-Hose' – in *Ways of Seeing*.

2 | FOUNDING FATHERS

Look back in nostalgia: Richard Hoggart

Though Richard Hoggart and Raymond Williams had never met before the publication of their first major works, the parallels between these two writers were striking even then. Both had been 'scholarship boys', coming to higher education from working-class childhoods in Leeds, England, and Abergavenny in Wales respectively, and thus 'marginalised' from birth in a way that Arnold and Leavis never were. Both went on to work as tutors of adult education with students who did not necessarily fit the university 'type', and so retained their contact with popular culture, even subculture, rather than the Leavisite elite.

Hoggart's *The Uses of Literacy* and Williams' *Culture and Society*, published within a year of each other in 1957 and 1958, shared similar concerns – the loss of an old culture and the threats, or challenges, of the new. Hoggart and Williams, by turning the close analysis of literary criticism onto popular texts – although neither is without an axe to grind on aspects of contemporary culture – embody a move beyond *Culture and Environment*, shaking off much of the pessimism and cynicism towards the popular that Leavis espoused and earning the label 'left-Leavisite'. Both writers' influence on cultural studies was immense. To take just the most obvious example, without Hoggart's founding of the Birmingham Centre for Contemporary Cultural Studies the discipline, such as it was, may well have floundered and died in the 1960s and this would be a far shorter book; more generally, these two texts became reading-list staples, were widely used for teaching and directly inspired a generation of students who would never previously have seen popular texts afforded this kind of cultural value or academic attention.

Finally, and fortunately, Hoggart and Williams have in common an accessible style which often makes their work a pleasure to engage with. Williams' writing, while sometimes austere, has at its best a lyrical passion and Hoggart's prose falls somewhere between novelistic description and the fluid rhetoric of a pub regular.

Richard Hoggart was born in 1918 to a working-class family in Chapeltown, Leeds. His father, then his mother died before he was seven years old and he was moved to his grandmother's house, while his sister and brother went to live with other relatives. Performing well in exams, he gained a place at grammar school and eventually a scholarship to Leeds University, where he studied English. He served in the Army as an anti-tank Captain during the Second World War and from 1946 to 1959 returned to Britain to teach literature on the adult education programme at the University of Hull. Following the publication of *The Uses of Literacy* in 1957, Hoggart became Professor of English at Birmingham, England, and in 1964 set up the Centre for Contemporary Cultural Studies, aided by Stuart Hall and partly financed, according to some reports, by Penguin Books in gratitude for his role in the Lady Chatterley trial – although Hoggart refers to this story as a 'ridiculous canard'. He remained the founding-director of the Centre until 1968, when he took the post of assistant director-general at UNESCO. With his eightieth birthday behind him, Richard Hoggart is still active today.

The Uses of Literacy (1957)

Simon During, in his *Cultural Studies Reader*, aptly describes *The Uses of Literacy* as a 'schizophrenic' book. It is a book in two minds about its project, and it is also, very much, a book of two halves.

By his own account, Hoggart set out to write the second half first. It was to engage with the contemporary 'mass' culture of the 1950s, in the manner of the Leavises' earlier accounts, and the working title was *The Abuses of Literacy*. The passion for autobiography which would lead Hoggart to write three volumes of memoirs must have taken over, for he pushed the account of modern culture into second place and filled five chapters with a description of the life he had grown up into; that is, the working-class industrial community of Leeds in the 1920s and 1930s. Titled 'An Older Order' and 'Yielding Place To New' respectively, these two sections perpetuate the contrast Leavis had made between 'good folk' and 'bad mass' cultures, with the important distinction that Hoggart's idealised past is far more recent than Leavis' nineteenth-century rural utopia and consequently celebrates a grubbily home-made, urban culture which both Leavis and Adorno would have disdained – and Arnold feared.

The full rich life

'I am from the working-classes ...' Hoggart declares his position early on in *The Uses of Literacy* and to his credit, states upfront both that he may exhibit a nostalgic bias and that he will try to overcome it in the interests of objectivity. It would be difficult to say that he succeeds; one of the lingering impressions of the book's first half is of grimy detail transformed into quite lovely prose, of anecdotes shown in with the words 'I remember'. At odd points Hoggart almost drifts into reverie with the kind of personal admission which is still rare in an academic text – 'if I hear *Valencia* or *I Left My Heart In Avalon* nowadays, no matter how played, I hear it poignantly as the street-pianos played it' – and the lengthy examination of this working-class culture through the eyes of an eleven-year-old boy clearly escapes the bounds of objective analysis and becomes quasi-autobiographical fiction.

> There are the varieties of light he will know: the sun forcing its way down as far as the ground-floor windows on a very sunny afternoon, the foggy grey of November over the slates and chimneys, the misty evenings of March when the gangs congregate in the watery yellow light of the kicked and scratched gas-lamp. Or the smells: the beer-and-Woodbine smell of the men on Saturday nights, the cheap powder-and-cream smell of his grown-up sisters, fish-and-chips ... **(64)**

There is a sensual potency in this writing which matches passages of George Orwell's and calls to mind the similarly vivid flashbacks of the Kinks or the Smiths, but it does not inspire confidence as a documentary account. The first section pivots on Hoggart's trust in his own personal experience as a guide to the universal cultural milieu, and while this may be considered more 'authentic' than Leavis' dependence on secondary sources for his portrait of 'organic' culture, it sometimes strains credibility too far, as when Hoggart insists that every working-class neighbourhood has 't'moor' nearby, 'a clinkered six-acre stretch surrounded by works and grimy pubs, with a large brick urinal at its edge' (59), or states simply that 'working-class girls are often very pretty' (128).

The oral tradition

Part of Hoggart's project is to represent working-class attitudes – towards authority, hardship, outsiders, sex and so on – through a recreation of their speech-patterns and characteristic phrases. So we are given lists of phrases which Hoggart recalls or in one case claims to have 'collected ... from a bright, pastel-shade distempered and tubular furnished waiting-room of a children's clinic [where] the conversation dribbled on aimlessly' – again, Hoggart is far more interested in descriptive prose than the conventions of ethnography. These snatches, flavouring the book's first half, suggest a superstition, a closing of ranks against difference and a common-sense 'wisdom': 'Unger's t'best sauce', 'I don't believe in doctors', 'Ah can't abide these *keen* women', 'British is best when y'come to it', 'Y've got to tek life as it cums.' Hoggart's own view of this mentality is not entirely favourable; he describes the 'dull fatalism' evident in the litany of banal phrases about 'meking do', the exclusion faced by anyone who criticises or crosses a social taboo, including the mistrust of 'book-learning', and the unquestioning ignorance about wider political issues. This last passage, where Hoggart typifies working-class views on religion and politics as 'a bundle of largely unexamined and orally-transmitted-tags, enshrining generalisations, prejudices and half-truths' (103) could be seen as a prejudiced generalisation itself, at the very least patronising, and certainly no proof of his assertion that 'most working-class people ... are non-metaphysical in their outlook. The important things in life, so far as they can see, are other things.'

For the most part, though, Hoggart's take on the oral culture of this community avoids both romanticism and distaste, retaining a healthy ambivalence by remembering the mixture of gentleness and savagery in his grandmother's generation and his own discovery that he had to modify the unwittingly abrupt habits of his speech in the world outside Leeds, holding back the 'short sharp jabs that are meant to go home – and yet not really meant to hurt' (88).

Working-class art

Like the other theorists discussed so far, Hoggart – having sketched his setting, or what he calls his 'landscape with figures' – goes on to identify what he considers 'good' culture. The culture he champions here is very different, though, from the *avant-garde* of Adorno, the Great Tradition or even Leavis' organic, rural culture. While he does link it to a literary heritage – of Moll Flanders, Chaucer's Wife of Bath and Shakespeare's bawdy women such as Juliet's nurse – Hoggart is extolling the virtues of a raucous lived culture which he finds in the group trip to the seaside, the fairground and the outing by 'chara', that is, a big bus. In a social sphere far removed from Leavis' quietly dignified labourers, here we have 'a great deal of loud laughter – at Mrs Johnson insisting on a paddle with her dress tucked in her bloomers, at Mrs Henderson pretending she has "got off" with the deck-chair attendant, or in the queue for the ladies' lavatory' (148). Also qualifying for Hoggart's grand old tradition of 'working-class art' are the pub and club singers with their tearful ballads and cheeky ditties, all of which Hoggart insists on listing at length – 'Hello, Hello, who's your Lady-friend?' ('It wasn't the girl I saw you with at Brighton ...') – and the picture-papers, such as *Thomson's Weekly News*, packed with romance stories and advertisements for miracle cures.

Three points should be drawn from this selection. Firstly, note that Hoggart's 'working-class art' is a culture of the people, generated bottom-up as opposed to Adorno's culture industry which imposes top-down, although in this respect we might dispute whether singalongs and days out can be considered in the same light as magazines 'produced by ... large commercial organisations'. Secondly, it can be observed that there is a strong female element to much of this culture, certainly in the implied audience of the magazines and in the cheerful antics of Mrs Henderson and her friends at the seaside, which can be contrasted to the almost exclusively 'masculine' tradition of honest toil and country lore dreamed up by Leavis. Finally, although my brief account above doesn't make it obvious, all Hoggart's descriptions of these worthy, jolly, cultural pursuits contain the seed of their bad opposite, the insipid taste of a 'modern' culture which threatens the old ways. The magazine stories of a comparatively innocent 'fall into sin' are defined against the later 'sex-and-violence novelettes', the collective singalong is compared favourably to the self-indulgent American style of crooning and even at the fairground Hoggart bemoans the loss of the carved merry-go-round horses against the increase in 'Coney Island-style coloured lights'. At this point the distinction between Leavis and Hoggart begins to erode; they may not agree on what they like, but both know what they don't like and it comes from across the Atlantic.

A candy-floss world

The move from past to present in *The Uses of Literacy* is, as John Docker has put it in *Postmodernism and Popular Culture*, a sudden shift from light to darkness, from cultural richness to poverty. 'The newer mass art' of popular journalism, fiction, even of singing, has a cynical and cheapening effect on the working-class culture Hoggart has described so lovingly. While it appeals to the working-class sense of dignity and community, it exploits these values into a surly pride – from 'Ah'm as good as you' to

'Yer no better than me' – and a herd-instinct which distrusts anything challenging or different. The ideal proposed by this new culture is the 'common man', the 'little man', the 'ordinary man'; Joe Normal with his wife and family. Its enemies are the fuddy-duddy 'highbrows' of literature, the 'cissies' of art, the 'do-gooders' and 'spotty-faced students' of education. It is a world of levelling-down, of 'syndicated ordinariness', of a stolidly unpretentious mass bound into a vast, false community by national magazines and broadcast television programmes. It is a constant present, a living for the shallow pleasure of the moment which glorifies the gang mentality of youth and mocks anything 'old-fashioned', traditional or bound up with history.

The voice of this new culture is 'cheeky', with what Hoggart sees as all the nerve and radicalism of a schoolboy who makes faces behind a copper's back and from a safe distance. He presents it in the style of the tabloid headlines and editorials: 'Nark it, chums', 'Pipe down on these stupid by-laws', 'Blimey, that sure is fighting talk'. It is fragmentary and bitty, typified by the magazine subheads 'Looked at lovely ladies – Lost his overcoat' and 'She likes to sing – in her scanties'; it is made up of teases and coy innuendo, such as the pin-up girls showing just 'the little bump of the nipples' or carefully lit to reveal a cleavage through nylon. In a sense this false cultural community, standardised, centralised and foisted on an audience who, while not cultural dopes, are characterised as particularly 'open' and 'vulnerable' to exploitation, echoes that described by Adorno. Perhaps more intriguingly, some of the qualities Hoggart identifies in this new mass culture – a shallowness and lack of affect, a reliance on the visual, an ignoring of history in favour of a fragmented eternal present – are exactly those which subsequent debate would call postmodern.

As those debates would also recognise, the purest form of this shallow, fragmentary aesthetic has its source in America, with British culture absorbing and incorporating it into a home-grown brand. Hoggart devotes himself to comparing the older, British tradition with its soggy romance and unspoken 'sins'– what he calls the Pierre Laforgue novel – to the far greater evils of the spicy, sex and violence novelette in the American gangster mould and quotes from both at length, for contrast:

At that moment she was intensely feminine.
'You are all mine, my darling. How I love you,' he murmured.
There was no hesitation, no shame and no regret in her soul as she
led him silently towards the bedroom …

All at once her body was pressing firm and yet trembling against me under that scanty dress. I could feel every line and curve of her. How hard can a girl press up to a guy, brother?

I started to open her dress fiercely … she showed me how, inbetween a mixture of whimpers and passionate gasps. And then … we met, like a pair of savage animals. (261)

You can see his point: but the curious thing, unremarked on by most commentators, is that Hoggart makes all these examples up. Even Pierre Laforgue, which Hoggart uses as a label for an entire genre, is simply an on the spot invention. Given the skill and enthusiasm of his pastiches – 'then her negligee – that split like a burst sheath', 'So I whipped my belt off and strapped her arms to the bedhead' – coupled with the intense detail in his description of pin-up girls, it is hard not to wonder whether Hoggart doesn't find at least a grudging pleasure in these modern texts.

Problems with Hoggart

Hoggart makes little attempt at any exact, rigorous analysis, trusting instead to his memories, opinions and his persuasive flair. The first section transforms his own subjective recollections into a 'documentary' account of working-class culture; the second pulls off the remarkable trick of closely analysing mass-market texts which the author makes up as he goes along. By contemporary standards, this would of course be unthinkable, but Hoggart's winning style encourages you to forgive him.

One point which commentators on *The Uses of Literacy* invariably question is Hoggart's portrayal of the youth produced by this Americanised mass culture. This is the now notorious 'milk-bar' passage, in which we see

boys … with drape-suits, picture ties and an American slouch. Most of them cannot afford a succession of milk-shakes, and make cups of tea serve for an hour or two whilst … they put copper after copper into the mechanical record-player. […] The young men waggle one shoulder or stare, as desperately as Humphrey Bogart, across the tubular chairs.

As many critics have pointed out, this constitutes the most irresponsible extreme of Hoggart's careless approach: rather than making any attempt to interview or engage with these boys, Hoggart condemns them from a distance through guess-work and emotive language, relying on a lazy style not far removed from the novelettes he has just criticised. Despite the attacks on this passage, Hoggart stands by his description, stating in a

1994 interview that 'it may be over-rhetorical, a bit over the top, but it's basically right'. Dick Hebdige, as discussed below, would certainly disagree.

Further reading

Hoggart's essays are collected in two volumes, *Speaking to Each Other: About Society* and *Speaking to Each Other: About Literature*, both published by Chatto and Windus in 1970. He has published three volumes of autobiography, also in Chatto and Windus editions: *A Local Habitation* (1988), *A Sort of Clowning* (1990) and *An Imagined Life* (1992). His most recent work to date is *The Way We Live Now* (1995).

The interview discussed above appears in *Conversations with Critics*, edited by Nicolas Tredell (Carcanet, 1994); another interview, with a discussion by Mark Gibson of 'Richard Hoggart's Grandmother's Ironing', was published in the flagship issue of the *International Journal of Cultural Studies* (Sage, 1998). Most books on cultural studies will include a treatment of Hoggart's work: the passage on *The Uses of Literacy* in John Docker's *Postmodernism and Popular Culture* (Cambridge University Press, 1994) is not particularly long but I think particularly canny.

One connection not always made is that between Hoggart and George Orwell. Orwell's 'The Decline of the English Murder', first published in 1946, strongly echoes Hoggart's distaste for American pulp fiction as opposed to the somehow more 'decent' English crime novel; in turn, Hoggart's portrayal of the working-class community in *The Uses of Literacy* finds parallels in Orwell's *Road to Wigan Pier* (1937). Dick Hebdige's short chapter 'A Negative Consensus' in *Hiding In The Light* (1988), is a pithy account of these similarities.

Devotees of the Richard Hoggart prose style will find the tradition continued regularly in his son Simon Hoggart's columns for the *Guardian*.

Links in this book

Both Hoggart and Williams are central nodes on a network which touches most of the writers in this book – rather than Six Degrees of Richard Hoggart, we would usually only need one or two. Of course, he was closely linked to Stuart Hall and the early work of the Birmingham Centre, although a recent interview suggests an intriguing ambivalence to this relationship. Hoggart claims never to have quarrelled with Hall himself but reports that by the late 1960s at least one student declared that the Centre no longer had time for the 'Matthew Arnoldian liberal humanism of Hoggart' and was advocating an exclusive left-wing membership which Hoggart thought illiberal. In the same discussion, Hoggart dismisses research on motorcycle gangs in Birmingham as 'romanticism'; he names no names but this can only be a reference to the 'youth culture' work of Paul Willis.

Looking to the other direction, F.R. Leavis' faintly snide comment on *The Uses of Literacy* was – again, according to Hoggart – 'he should have written a novel', while his wife apparently complained before her death that Hoggart and Williams had 'climbed on the back of her work and made themselves fortunes from it'. Hoggart in turn saw *The Uses of Literacy* as an improvement on Q.D. Leavis' *Fiction and the Reading Public*, which he felt held working-class culture at arm's length: 'Mrs Leavis and the Dangers of Narrowness', in the first volume of *Speaking to Each Other*, politely lists her other flaws and suggests *Culture and Society* as a corrective.

A feeling for change: Raymond Williams

Raymond Williams was born in 1921, in the rural Welsh village of Pandy, Abergavenny; his father was a railway signalman. He was educated at the local school and won a scholarship to Trinity College, Cambridge, where his background marked him as an outsider. Williams taught in adult education from 1946 to 1960 and became involved with the journal *Politics and Letters*, which united Leavisite criticism with left-wing, working-class politics. These experiences fed directly into his first major book, *Culture and Society 1780–1950* (1958). *The Long Revolution* followed in 1961, by which time Williams was lecturing at Cambridge. He wrote articles and reviews for the *Guardian*, *Tribune* and the *Listener* and continued to publish within what was then the nascent discipline of cultural studies, continuing his project on technology and cultural change in *Communications* (1962) and contributing to the media research ongoing at Birmingham and elsewhere with *Television: Technology and Cultural Form* in 1974.

From 1974 to 1983 Williams was Professor of Drama at Cambridge, a post which reflected his investment in literary criticism, yet he continued to refine his own position on cultural studies and engage with change as it occurred; one of his last works, published in 1983 – which should have finally given the lie to his reputation for nostalgia – was *Towards 2000*.

Raymond Williams died in 1988.

Culture and Society (1958), *The Long Revolution* (1961)

Raymond Williams' project, like Richard Hoggart's, is very much concerned with the past – with the varied histories of cultural criticism, education, the novel, standard English, the reading public and the popular press – but rather than cordoning off a stage in cultural history as an 'ideal' to compare favourably with the current state of society, Williams treats history as a process whereby cultural forms shape and are shaped by the wider context of their period and then crucially applies the same model to his own contemporary society of the early 1960s. Through a re-evaluation and debunking of received ideas about historical progress and change, Williams is able by extension to challenge the myths about modern 'mass' culture and perform an analysis far more objective than any we have seen so far of the relationship between contemporary cultural forms – the press, advertising and the novel, for instance – and the cultural position he is writing from.

Williams sees this position as a pivotal one, a key point in the 'long revolution' from which society can choose its paths, either towards further positive change or to cultural stagnation. He argues that society is already becoming trapped by notions of class boundaries, of economic value and profit motive, while political alternatives or genuine proposals for different strategies either lose their edge and fade into the dominant system or are mistrusted and labelled 'extremist.' In the face of this worryingly invulnerable yet ultimately self-defeating status quo, Williams offers his own suggestions as to how society could recover the sense of community, common purpose and shared investment in culture which he is sure it needs, including – again, in contrast to all the critics we have surveyed so far – a fair-minded embracing of new technologies and a belief in the potential of new cultural forms.

A common heritage

Culture and Society is largely taken up with the account of critical history whose rationale I borrowed for my Introduction: a general enquiry into ways of thinking about culture, but built around 'particular thinkers and their actual statements'. Williams' purpose here is to explore this heritage of ideas and through it to encourage reflection and change.

The tradition it records is a major contribution to our common understanding, and a major incentive to its necessary extensions. There are ideas, and ways of thinking, with the seeds of life in them, and there are others, perhaps deep in our minds, with the seeds of a general death. Our measure of success in recognising these kinds, and in naming them making possible their common recognition, may literally be the measure of our future. (338)

We can note here a number of themes which resurface throughout both *Culture and Society* and *The Long Revolution*: the image of two paths, one to a progressive future and one to a spiritual death, the importance of commonality and collective understanding, of recognising a shared history and a shared responsibility, and with the even-handed ambivalence typical of Williams, an openness to the 'good' and 'bad' aspects of every cultural period. While others revered the past as a lost kingdom, Williams chose to re-evaluate rather than reminisce and found just about as much that was affirming and as much which was harmful in the 1840s as he did in the 1950s.

The main body of *Culture and Society* examines the way 'key words' – 'industry', 'democracy', 'art', 'class' and 'culture' – were used and how their usage changed, through three historical phases. The first, comprising nineteenth century thought, includes John Stuart Mill, Jeremy Bentham, Samuel Taylor Coleridge and Matthew Arnold; the second is a brief 'interregnum' crossing the two centuries which brings in T.E. Hulme and George Bernard Shaw and the last considers, among others, D.H. Lawrence, T.S. Eliot, F.R. Leavis and George Orwell. It is significant that while Williams' project in this book is very much one of 'cultural studies', it is built upon a tradition of novelists, poets and literary critics, again demonstrating very clearly where the heritage of this discipline lies.

Offering a kind of 'Teach Yourself Arnold', Williams questions assumptions about each writer and challenges the assertions of the theorists themselves. He comes down hard, for instance, against Arnold's stratification of class groupings – 'it offered category feelings about human behaviour, based on a massing and simplifying of actual individuals, as an easy substitute for the difficulties of personal and immediate judgement' – and asks searching questions of Arnold's all-powerful 'State'. Where were its members to come from? How was its project of achieving 'perfection' going to tally with the personal interests and powers of those who controlled it? Ultimately, Williams identifies the 'maximum of order' which this State was to embody as a fearful and potentially tyrannical response to the perceived threat of the working classes, who to Arnold were a looting, rowdy mob but to Williams a non-violent movement seeking not to destroy society but to argue for change.

He is equally firm, though fair, with Leavis. While praising *Culture and Environment*'s educational project of practical criticism, he diagnoses its comparisons between old and new as 'myth ... a surrender to a characteristically industrialist, or urban, nostalgia' and brusquely surmises that 'if there is one thing certain about "the organic community" it is that it has always gone'. That Leavis overlooks in his recreation of the 'organic' idyll all its obvious ills – 'the penury, the petty tyranny, the disease and mortality, the ignorance and frustrated intelligence which were also among its ingredients' – is condemned as 'foolish and dangerous'.

Similarly, Leavis' account of the flat, spiritually impoverished modern industrial lifestyle is taken apart and its generalisations laid bare. Can we really assert in all honesty, Williams asks, that all workers of our period see their daily labour as meaningless, that all their leisure activities are pointless and redundant? Williams, again distinguishing himself from both Leavis and Arnold by refusing to see these workers as a 'mass', persuasively shows that to make such assumptions about our own contemporaries is arrogant and inaccurate, especially when coupled with the belief that the culture's salvation lies in an educated 'minority' and the balm of great prose or poetry.

One of Leavis' key failings is to construct the 'organic' and the 'modern' lifestyles from the books of George Sturt – *Change in the Village* and *The Wheelwright's Shop* – juxtaposed with the nightmarish accounts of books like *Star-Dust In Hollywood*. By contrast, Williams insists that the state of a cultural period cannot be read solely from literary evidence, that the part cannot be taken for the whole. A culture and the experience of living in that culture is made up not just of the acclaimed works which survive but of its cheap entertainments, its documentary records, its miscellaneous artefacts and primary texts. It is through this holistic approach, as opposed to the Leavisite reliance on handy secondary accounts, that Williams attempts to reconstruct the cultural framework of a period, or what he calls its 'structure of feeling'.

Structures of feeling

> It is as firm and definite as 'structure' suggests, yet it operates in the most delicate and least tangible parts of our activity. In one sense, this structure of feeling is the culture of a period: it is the particular living result of all the elements in the general organisation. (48)

The precise meaning of Williams' 'structure of feeling' has remained notoriously difficult to pin down; even his original definition here suggests an attempt to catch a cloud. As the closest equivalent, we might suggest '*Zeitgeist*'. In practice what Williams means is the recovery of the genuine culture of a period – that is, the 'actual living sense, the deep community' – through the traces that remain of it. Once the community has passed on, we can reconstruct them through a forensic analysis of their 'documentary culture ... from poems to buildings and dress-fashions'.

Williams' definition of 'culture' here is, it should be noticed, very much wider than that of previous theorists and willingly embraces all kinds of pop and ephemera as valuable evidence; by extension it treats all communication media, including more recent forms such as advertising and cinema, as potentially useful and valid objects for study. Where a strict Leavisite would retain only an elite canon of great literary texts to stand for and represent the spirit of the times, Williams exposes this approach as a filtering process which he calls the 'selective tradition'. In order to recapture the genuine community or structure of feeling, we have to go beyond this snobbish 'best of' mentality and recover the forgotten texts – the also-ran novels, the letters, the wedding registers, pamphlets, voting polls and cartoons. By making links between these and the political and social history of a period, Williams attempts to sketch the 'social character' of a particular decade. Though his example here is the 1840s, the same open-handed approach applies equally to the 1960s, as he finds elements of the contemporary structure of feeling – isolation, alienation and self-exile – in Aldous Huxley's *Brave New World* and Orwell's *Nineteen Eighty-Four*.

'Mass' culture

You will remember that Adorno rejected the term 'mass culture' because it wasn't negative enough. Williams also finds the term problematic, but for different reasons. As we've seen, Williams regards the media of any period as essentially neutral, and their products as neither absolutely good nor bad. In his section on mass communication he again reminds the reader that every historical period leaves behind its gems as well as its

gewgaws, and urges a more objective historical perspective; just as the
rise of cheap paperbacks and tabloid newspapers might be despised in the
1950s as symptoms of creeping lower-class tastes, so the rise of the novel
in the 1730s was regarded at the time as a distasteful product of the
'vulgar' middle-class. Some of those novels may indeed have been
forgettable and have been forgotten. The same is true of modern culture.

> If there are many bad books, there are also an important number of
> good books ... if the readers of bad newspapers have increased in
> number, so have the readers of better newspapers and periodicals, so
> have the users of public libraries, so have students in all kinds of
> formal and informal adult education. (308)

The products of 'mass' communication which Hoggart despaired of are,
then, viewed by Williams as neither a blessing nor a curse; many of them,
at least compared with others of their type, 'have the merits at least of being
bright, attractive, popular'. Certainly, their means of transmission – the
technology of television and radio, for instance – is not harmful in itself.

Where Williams does see potential harm is in the actual terminology
'mass communication'. When we speak of masses, he argues, we assume
a lumpen majority of the type feared by Arnold. Historically, 'mass' came
to stand for 'mob', and so 'mass-thinking', 'mass-suggestion', 'mass-
prejudice', even 'mass-democracy' became terms of hostility, calling to
mind that gang of rioters who pulled down the Hyde Park railings in 1866.
Williams again speaks firmly. To talk of masses is to perpetuate a
prejudice and falsification; it is always to talk of the 'other', never
ourselves.

> I do not think of my relatives, friends, neighbours, colleagues,
> aquaintances as masses: we none of us can or do. Yet now, in our kind
> of society, we see these others regularly ... stand, physically, beside
> them. They are here, and we are here with them. There are in fact no
> masses; there are only ways of seeing people as masses. (299)

This is the voice of the young man from the Welsh border country who
refused to be intimidated by the culture of Cambridge and who puts to
shame all the prejudices handed down by Matthew Arnold.

The term 'communication' also needs to be interrogated. What we see
now, Williams argues, is in fact 'a failure to understand communication';
that is, the contemporary media fail to live up to the two-way process the
word implies, and instead provide merely 'transmission'. An attempt to

force knowledge from above onto a supposedly passive audience will meet only with sullen resistance. What is needed is a communication not of received 'facts' but of the desire to learn, of the tools to examine and challenge; rather than dominating and telling, modern communication should give open access to information and encourage the viewer to make his or her own choices. It is in this sense that Leavis' project in *Culture and Environment*, despite its prejudices, remains admirable to Williams.

Stagnation

The 'massification' Williams despairs of – seeing others as 'them' and selfishly caring only about individual prospects, rather than those of the whole community – is just one of the symptoms of a general social crisis. In accord with Adorno's take on Marxism, he argues that our economic system is focusing on the 'consumer' and profit value, to the extent that principles of genuine need and use value have been forgotten. What do we use a product for? Do we really need it? What effect does our use have on society as a whole? Rather than considering these fundamental issues, we tend to buy products for which the need has merely been created by market research and advertising, prompted by vague insecurities or fear of social inadequacy – 'You Need Pocket Radio' is Williams' inevitably dated example, but the same principle runs through John Berger's more recent examples and in a more subtle form, most contemporary advertising, just as it can be found in the advertising copy Leavis scathingly quotes and at another remove in Adorno's 'one simply "has to" have seen *Mrs Miniver*'.

In this increasing concern with the individual and blindness to our own role in a wider society Williams sees a dangerous false consciousness – epitomised in another of his examples by our reluctance to spend 'our' money on taxes to fund the social system without which, Williams argues, 'hardly any of us could get any money, or even live for more than a few days'. This mentality has flourished in the gaps left by our lack of community and failure to see a wider context beyond our own actions. If it is allowed to continue, he warns, our way of life will become increasingly selfish, our sense of community continue to wither and our way of seeing others become increasingly distorted. Williams' soothsaying sounds melodramatic until we remember that a mere two decades later the British premier announced, with no shame or regret, that there no longer existed such a thing as society. What followed must have confirmed Williams in his most pessimistic forecasts.

The common culture

'We need a common culture, not for the sake of an abstraction, but because we shall not survive without it,' Williams states in *Culture and Society*. We have seen something of his nightmare: what of his dream?

In general terms, he speaks of a common culture which values 'diversity in community'; a pride in one's own position coupled with respect for the very different skills and abilities of others. Gardening and carpentry – the kind of trades Leavis so admired as country 'lore' – should be regarded on a level with reading and study. A physicist would not be thought better than a composer or a chess-player. Realising the balance which would have to be achieved between increasing specialisation and a wider awareness of community, Williams proposes that the dilemma will be solved

> ... as a man becomes conscious that the value he places on his skill, the differentiation he finds in it, can only ultimately be confirmed by his constant effort not only to confirm and respect the skills of others, but to confirm and deepen the community which is even larger than the skills.

We might note that, caught up in this vision of masculine trade and labour, Williams seems to omit women from his hard-working community.

In *The Long Revolution* Williams develops his thesis further and offers more concrete proposals for a way out of the 'stagnation' he sees ahead: the funding both of artists and of criticism groups for the open discussion of their work; a network of publicly-owned theatres to be hired at their convenience by companies of actors; a government authority with the responsibility for funding film-making groups and running both popular and independent cinema chains; a Books Council to ensure that every town has a decent bookshop where minority as well as popular texts are readily available. In a way these suggestions may seem whimsical to us now, over-optimistic and unachievable: but again, only until we remember that shifts no more radical, but with the opposite effect – cuts rather than boosts in funding, the undermining rather than the encouragement of unions, a favouring of the mainstream and suspicion of 'alternative' media – were forced onto the arts during Margaret Thatcher's time in government. Indeed, re-reading *The Long Revolution* as I did on the day of the 1997 General Election, some thirty-six years since the book's publication, my feelings were not of scorn for his hopeless optimism but admiration for Williams' stubborn willingness to play the 'awkward squad', and a sense of wonder that despite these eminently reasonable suggestions and the accuracy of his warnings, nothing was done.

Problems with Williams

Some critics have accused Williams of failing to engage with a theoretical framework and employing too unfocused a method. While this seems overly harsh considering the position of these two books at the beginning of cultural studies rather than within an established discipline, there is perhaps something too vague and utopian about the description of a 'common culture' given above, with its mutually-respectful citizens and motley collection of 'skills'. Although, as I have indicated, I find many of Williams' suggestions for a shared and well-funded arts system entirely persuasive, he does not explain how the talents of a chess-player or gardener would immediately become more valuable within this system.

Secondly, and despite Williams' comparatively generous attitude towards most modern culture, there is evidence here again, albeit only occasional, of the kind of subjective divisions between good and bad which dominated the work of Adorno, Leavis and Hoggart. Football is 'a wonderful game', jazz and homemaking are important cultural forms, but the 'horror-film, the rape-novel, the Sunday strip-paper and the latest Tin-Pan drool are not exactly in the same world'. This list, with its substitution of garish style and caricature for accuracy – what is a 'rape-novel', after all? – is in the vein of Hoggart's worst moments and the distinction it makes is entirely arbitrary.

Further reading

Most of Williams' key works are listed above, but the first stop for a newcomer should not be these weighty texts but his short essay 'Culture Is Ordinary', first published in 1958 and collected in *Resources of Hope* (Verso, 1988). Plain-speaking and lyrical at once, this piece is reminiscent of Orwell at his most convincing and communicates powerfully the extent to which Williams' roots in Pandy affected his view of Cambridge.

Hoggart was told he should have written a novel; Williams went one better and has published half a dozen, in addition to plays and a handful of short stories. *Border Country* (1960) and *Second Generation* (1964) in particular call on the rural background which Williams refused to shake off.

The Stuart Hall piece mentioned immediately below appears in *Raymond Williams: Critical Perspectives*, edited by Terry Eagleton (Polity Press, 1989). Although Eagleton had previously subjected Williams' work to hostile critique, he is generous and celebratory here, although his criticism of Williams – for instance, his long *New Left Review* article of 1976, reprinted in *Criticism and Ideology* (1976) – is listed in the bibliography.

George Orwell's concerns and style are traceable in Williams' work just as they are in Hoggart and Williams makes no secret of his fascination. In addition to his section on Orwell in *Culture and Society*, he is author of the Fontana Modern Masters guide *Orwell*, published in 1971 with a revised edition in 1984, and edited *George Orwell: A Collection of Critical Essays* in 1974.

Links in this book

Williams' approach to Arnold and Leavis will now be apparent. Leavis for his part offered of *Culture and Society* the characteristically sour 'Queenie did it all in the Thirties'; both he and his wife, it seems, were unwilling to see Williams and Hoggart as anything other than upstarts, usurpers of their own approach.

Stuart Hall, who worked with Williams on the *May Day Manifesto* (Penguin, 1968) has stressed the parallel between Williams' alienation at Cambridge in the 1940s and his own entry, as a West Indian student, into Oxford a decade later. Both men, their confidence broken by the relentless class superiority of the place, shared a sense of Oxbridge as a 'colonial' experience.

3 IDEOLOGIES OF THE EVERYDAY

This chapter, on the work of Roland Barthes and John Berger, figures as a slight detour in the so far fairly linear journey from Arnold to Williams. Barthes is often omitted from accounts of cultural studies' history, while Berger is rarely mentioned. For several reasons, though, I think they provide a useful side route.

Barthes' *Mythologies* was first published in 1957 but translated into English in 1972, the year Berger's *Ways of Seeing* first appeared; the two books thus bridge the chronological gap between Hoggart and Williams' first major writing in the late 1950s and the first real shoots from the Birmingham School in the early 1970s. Both *Mythologies* and *Ways of Seeing* in effect continue the approach Williams was the first to embrace, that is, the study of popular, modern texts for their own sake, rather than in contrast to a superior canon, *avant-garde* or old organicism. In contrast to Arnold's vagueness, Adorno's lofty refusal to grubby himself with close analysis and Leavis and Hoggart's tendency to invent their own examples, Berger and Barthes share an intention to closely examine the visual language of contemporary culture. Through this close study they both mean to expose the ideological meanings of modern advertising, magazine photographs and journalism.

It must seem by now that I claim nearly every example here is accessible and readable in its way, but *Mythologies* and *Ways of Seeing* really are short, almost flimsy books despite their importance. *Ways of Seeing* is full of pictures and short, choppy instructions, while *Mythologies*, largely reprinted from Barthes' newspaper articles, retains its likeable chapter headings: 'Soap-powders and Detergents', 'Wine and Milk', and perhaps most endearing, 'Steak and Chips'. Both are in print and well worth reading.

Roland Barthes

Roland Barthes was born in 1915 to a comfortable French Protestant family in Cherbourg. His father died in action as a naval officer within a year and the boy was raised by his mother and grandparents within a milieu of bourgeois female company and culture, learning the piano from his aunt. In 1924 he and his mother moved to Paris, where Barthes studied towards the *baccalaureat* while his mother supported them both as a bookbinder.

Completing a degree in French, Latin and Greek, Barthes found teaching work in Paris at the end of the 1930s. He had been exempted from military service due to his emergent tuberculosis and a relapse in 1941 took him to a sanatorium in the Alps, where he spent the period of German occupation engaged in solitary reading and study. During the late 1940s and early 1950s Barthes continued to teach and pursue literary criticism, resulting in *Writing Degree Zero* of 1953 and the articles which would be collected and expanded in *Mythologies*.

In 1965 an attack on Barthes in particular as representative of a new irreverent criticism was published by the professor Raymond Picard, sparking a debate which soon brought Barthes a radical notoriety and, by the late 1960s, had made him something of a celebrity academic. He became associated with fellow Parisian theorists Claude Lévi-Strauss, Michel Foucault and Jacques Lacan, was internationally feted and began to take up requests for lecture tours. During the next decade Barthes published his major works, *S/Z* (1970) and *The Pleasure of the Text* (1973), in addition to a curious, possibly semi-fictional account of his life, *Roland Barthes by Roland Barthes* (1975), and a popular book on the sentimental language of lovers' 'discourse – in fragments'. In 1976 he took a professorial chair at the prestigious College de France and was by now considered an intellectual giant, his fame far exceeding academic circles.

In February 1980, crossing the street outside the College de France, Barthes was knocked down by a laundry truck, and died soon afterwards.

Mythologies (1957)

Like *The Uses of Literacy*, *Mythologies* falls into two distinct parts. The first is the collection of essays which first appeared in a series, 'Mythology of the Month', in the magazine *Les Lettres Nouvelles* between 1954 and 1956. In 1956, Barthes read the work of Ferdinand de Saussure, the Swiss linguist who had proposed a 'science of signs' which he called semiology, and the second section of *Mythologies*, titled 'Myth Today', is a long essay which appropriates and extends Saussure's theories, giving the analysis of myth a framework and structure which the earlier essays only feel for.

As this second section is by far the more 'difficult', it makes sense to deal primarily with 'Myth Today', using the shorter essays as illustration.

Semiology and language

Ferdinand de Saussure's model of language as a 'sign-system' is made up of three interconnected concepts: the signifier, the signified and the sign.

To take a simple and widely-used example, if I say the word 'cat' the sound I make, which can be written /cat/, is the signifier. The concept I am referring to, which you may see in your mind's eye as a <<cat>>, a domestic feline, is the signified. The relation between the two, which in English usually guarantees that when I say /cat/ you know I mean <<cat>>, is the sign.

We should remember that this last relationship is purely arbitrary. We could in theory use any word to signify <<cat>> as long as it didn't risk confusion with other signs; 'dat' would work equally well, for instance, but 'bat', 'hat' or 'dog' would not. Similarly, the link between /cat/ and the concept of a domestic feline works in English but would not be so readily made in Germany or Italy – although speakers used to *die Katze* and *il Gatto* might well make the connection – and would fall entirely flat in Iraq or Siberia.

The simple model can be complicated further if we remember that a signifier can be linked to several signifieds at once, although this doesn't usually pose a problem in speech: if I say /cat/ you will work out from the context whether I mean a domestic feline, a knotted whip or a type of boat. Finally, a signified concept can potentially be connected to more than one signifier; in French, for instance, the image of a domestic feline is suggested equally by *le chat* and *la chatte*.

While de Saussure constructed this framework around linguistic communication, it has proved equally useful in other fields. Barthes himself gives the example of Freud's dream-interpretation, wherein the signifier is the 'manifest' content, or the way the dream seems to us, the signified is the 'latent', or true content as revealed by the psychoanalyst, and the sign is the 'dream-work', the total process which disguises our daily concerns as night-time narratives.

Prepare for level two:

Myth as a metalanguage

What Barthes does is build on this signifier-signified-sign model and extend it to another level. Myth, he says, is constructed 'from a semiological chain which existed before it: it is a second-order semiological system.' Rather than a normal language in which that /cat/, <cat> equation worked, it is a metalanguage, a language which speaks about language.

This calls for another illustration and, as we're talking about metalanguage now, we may as well graduate from my 'cat' model to Barthes' example about a lion.

Barthes imagines himself back in the second form at school, reading a sentence in his Latin grammar text: '*quia ego nominor leo*'. On the first level of linguistic meaning, the pupil makes sense of those signifiers, the written words on a page, and understands a simple meaning, a signifier: 'because my name is lion'. As a quotation from Aesop's fables which would be well-known to a French child of the 1920s, the line already has a rich series of connotations, as Barthes demonstrates: 'I am an animal, a lion, I live in a certain country, I have just been hunting, they would have me share my prey with a heifer, a cow and a goat; but being the stronger, I award myself all the shares for various reasons, the last of which is quite simply that my name is lion.' Hence the phrase 'the lion's share'.

But as an example in a Latin phrasebook, all this meaning is placed at a distance. It doesn't matter why the lion said it, what the preceding story was; the point here is, as the pupil realises, to illustrate the grammatical agreement of the predicate. The meaning of the written words '*quia ego nominor leo*', which was a signified within the linguistic model, is seen to be part of a larger, second-order structure.

'Because my name is lion', within this second structure, has really got nothing to do with lions. What it signifies is 'I am a grammatical example' and it is tied up with general cultural notions of French education, of the continued teaching of Latin, of the streaming which would face only the brighter pupils with a Latin textbook. This is what Barthes calls the 'mythical' level, the level of cultural connotations rather than simple linguistic meanings.

Myth as politicised speech

The example of the lion taking his share from the heifer, goat and cow, then being turned into a grammatical exercise, may illustrate myth as a second-order system but may not otherwise seem particularly significant

– although Barthes notes wryly that the lion himself might feel differently, stressing the 'jurisprudence which leads him to claim a prey because he is the strongest, unless we deal with a bourgeois lion ...'

Barthes' other example makes his point about myth more strongly. Now he sees himself in the barber's, looking at the cover of a *Paris-Match* on which a black soldier in the French military uniform is apparently saluting the tricolour flag. On the first level of signification, we read the pattern of printed shapes and colours on the cover as signifying a black man in a French uniform. Like the lion, this signified concept has a rich history behind it – this particular man joined the army for a series of reasons, he probably has a family, he may have been obliged to take French rather than Latin at school, he may be thinking about his supper as he salutes.

Within the second-order system of myth, though, all this is pushed away and held at a distance. The black-soldier-saluting-the-flag, which we read on a literal level as a signified, doubles as a signifier on the next level. What does he signify? As Barthes puts it, perhaps in the voice of the barber, 'The French Empire? It's just a fact: look at this good Negro who salutes like one of our own boys.' He signifies a nation which assimilates different cultures into a patriotic fighting force, a great Empire with loyal colonies and devoid of racial discrimination. He signifies a myth of French Imperialism to comfort the readers of *Paris-Match*.

So the man himself has been appropriated, lifted out of his real history and personality and used as an icon, an abstract signifier. The reality of his existence has been, to use Barthes' various metaphors, held at a distance, frozen, numbed – but not completely removed. The myth needs the real man to retain its power of objective 'truth' ('it's just a fact: look at this good Negro'), as we can see if we imagine the diminished potency a drawing of the same subject would have.

It is clear that this myth serves some more than others. It is a myth of reassurance and comfort for the French middle-classes, or more accurately those 'petty-bourgeois' who aspire to middle-class values. It works through naturalisation, through making itself seem like common-sense ('it's just a fact'), through hiding the artifice which goes into the process of myth-making. Successful myth must seem 'obvious', rather than opinion.

In this way cultural mythology has, in recent history, made it seem 'obvious' that rising immigration means greater unemployment, that the British royal family are marvellous national figureheads, that gay men spread AIDS, that a Labour government would be under the thumb of the trade unions. Traditionally, Barthes argues, myth has been on the side of the politically right wing – under the guise, crucially, of 'depoliticised', naturalised, common-sense – as it requires a tight control on cultural production. The voice of the oppressed, the colonial or the minority declares itself as such rather than passing itself off as 'obvious'; which is not to say that when the 'Left' does gain power it can't be just as adept as its former opponents at producing fully naturalised mythologies of its own.

Mythologist at work

The work of the mythologist, then – that is, the analyst, rather than the producer of myths – is to perform a trick of focusing both on the cultural connotations of a myth and on the other, more literal meaning which myth attempts to subsume. The myth of red wine in France, for instance, is tied up with unpretentious manly enjoyment and the partaking of a shared national pleasure, to the extent that a politician photographed with a bottle of beer in front of him alienates himself in that moment from the common culture; yet Barthes perceives that while 'wine is a good and fine substance, it is no less true that its production is deeply involved in French capitalism' and leads directly to the exploitation of Muslim workers.

This is the project of *Mythologies'* main body: a deciphering of the myths which inhabit steak as virile national emblem, the new Citroën as classical architecture, children's toys as preparation for bourgeois adult life, Omo and Persil as different methods of cleansing despite their shared origin in the multinational Unilever. Although Barthes tackles it with enthusiasm, his task is a lonely one: as he states plainly in a passage which could also speak for Adorno's scathing analysis of his own society, the cultural critic is condemned to stand outside the world he analyses.

> The mythologist cuts himself off from all the myth-consumers, and this is no small matter. If this applied to a particular section of the collectivity, well and good. But when a myth reaches the entire community, it is from the latter than the mythologist must become estranged if he wants to liberate the myth. [...] To decipher the Tour de France or the 'good French wine' is to cut oneself off from those who are entertained or warmed up by them. (157)

Yet despite Barthes' melancholy portrait of the mythologist, whose only 'connection with the world is of the order of sarcasm', his popularity in fact soared during his lifetime far beyond mere academic appreciation and his lectures attracted crowds of tourists as well as members of his own

Parisian community. Perhaps the self-deprecation and wit of his accounts endeared him to his readership despite the fears he voices above; or perhaps, like Adorno, he underestimated the potential of those he calls 'myth-consumers' to decipher and analyse for themselves.

Problems with Barthes

Some have dismissed Barthes' critique as dated and no longer relevant. Certainly the 'bourgeoisie' he attacks is a specifically French class of a specific historical moment; it is hard to know what this might mean within other national cultures during the late 1990s. However, Michael Moriarty reminds us in *Roland Barthes*, detailed below, that Barthes' analysis 'is not as dated as some might think, and others wish', pointing to Barthes' attack on the right-wing populist Poujade and his follower Jean-Marie Le Pen, who currently heads the French National Front.

More specifically, I implied above that the first section of *Mythologies*, in all its playfulness, lacks the theoretical structure which 'Myth Today' develops. This is to be expected, but some of the articles seem to actively contradict the later essay. In the most obvious instance, the chapter on 'The World of Wrestling' which heads *Mythologies* immerses itself in the theatricality and spectacle of popular wrestling, apparently taking great pleasure in what are excessive, mythical archetypes and iconic performances; that is, going against the grain of what Barthes later defines as the mythologist's duty. Of course, there is a distinction between these magazine pieces and the post-Saussurian essay, but we might expect that, having struggled through 'Myth Today', the lighter articles would provide consistent examples of the theory.

Further reading

Apart from *Mythologies* itself, a good introduction to Barthes' semiological analysis is the essay 'Rhetoric of the Image' which takes as its example a spaghetti advertisement as embodiment of 'Italianicity'. First published in the journal *Communications* in 1964, it now appears in *Image-Music-Text*, edited by Stephen Heath (Fontana, 1977).

Barthes' other works, as mentioned above, include *Writing Degree Zero* (1953), *S/Z* (1970) – Barthes' famous structuralist analysis of the Balzac story 'Sarrasine' – *The Pleasure of the Text* (1973) and *Camera Lucida* (1980), writings on photography prompted by the death of his mother in 1977. Additional essays, which were untranslated in the original English version of *Mythologies*, appear in *The Eiffel Tower and Other Mythologies*, edited by Richard Howard (Hill and Wang, 1979).

I have given the English translations in every case here for convenience, but of course these texts did not usually appear under these titles in the same year as the French publication.

I have found John Culler's *Barthes* (Fontana Modern Masters, 1983) an excellent resource and Michael Moriarty's *Roland Barthes* (Polity Press, 1991) is a useful although more dense and complex account.

Culler has also written an equally clear and concise Modern Masters text on Ferdinand de Saussure, which I would recommend to those making further exploration into semiology.

In a different vein, Joan Smith's *Misogynies* (Faber, 1989), a collection of journalistic accounts on the portrayal of women in a variety of cultural forms, explicitly pays tribute to Barthes and offers an interesting, late-1980s feminist parallel to *Mythologies*.

Not further reading exactly, but the films of Jean-Luc Godard are in many ways a cinematic equivalent to Barthes' mix-and-match musings on Parisian culture: though a product of the 1960s rather than the 1950s, *Two Or Three Things I Know About Her* is perhaps the nearest thing to *Mythologies* on film.

Links in this book

While he shared his cultural moment with Michel Foucault, Barthes' analysis of the smallest details of French taste shares more of its flavour with Pierre Bourdieu's *Distinction* than the works of Foucault discussed in this book. His project to expose 'naturalised', invisible bourgeois ideology in contemporary images clearly gives him much in common with John Berger's modern Marxism and, in turn, with Stuart Hall's view of dominant ideology's insidious, persuasive power in British cultural life of the 1960s and 1970s.

John Berger

Born in London on Guy Fawkes' night, 1926, John Berger was sent as a boy to a harsh prep school and then to an equally savage public school. At the age of sixteen he ran away, gained a scholarship and entered the Central School of Art, where his latent anarchist beliefs were hardened into communism. He was forced into the Army and spent two years as an instructor, coming into close contact with working-class men for the first time. On a grant from the Army he resumed his studies at the Chelsea School of Art, and became more closely involved with the Communist Party.

During the early 1950s Berger continued to paint while working at a factory in Croydon; he subsequently taught art for the Workers' Educational Association, gave radio talks for the BBC West African Service and wrote for the *New Statesman*. In addition to works of art criticism on Picasso, Berger also produced four novels during the 1950s and 1960s: *A Painter of Our Time*, *The Foot of Clive*, *Corker's Freedom* and *A Fortunate Man*, the latter his first collaboration with the photographer Jean Mohr. His next two works were *Art and Revolution* and the novel *G*, which won the Booker Prize for fiction in 1972; a controversial decision made more so by Berger's announcement that half his prize money of £5,000 would be donated to the Black Panthers.

In the same year, *Ways of Seeing* was released in Britain as a four-part, late night television programme on BBC2, a channel noted for its public service, arts and education broadcasting. Intended partly as a reaction and riposte to Kenneth Clark's grandiose art series *Civilisation*, *Ways of Seeing* won a small but dedicated audience and was repeated during prime time. The book which followed quickly became a bestseller and a key text in art colleges across the UK and United States.

In 1974 Berger moved to a small peasant community in France, where he began work on his trilogy *Into Their Labours*. This work, consisting of the novels *Pig Earth*, *Once in Europa* and *Lilac and Flag*, was only recently completed.

John Berger continues to live in the French Alps.

Ways of Seeing (1972)

Ways of Seeing is a formally unusual text in several ways. It was based on the BBC television series of the same name and, while it now stands as a book in its own right, on its publication in 1972 it was the book-of-the-series, what might be called a spin-off or more favourably, an integral but incomplete part of the multi-media project that was 'Ways of Seeing'. Secondly, while John Berger is credited on the spine, cover and title page of the book, four other joint authors are named less prominently. As with Denys Thompson's contribution to *Culture and Environment* and, indeed, with some of Stuart Hall's collectively edited volumes, we have little way of knowing which writer wrote what. While the 'selective tradition' has remembered this as a book 'by John Berger', then – a convention I am following, as shorthand, throughout this chapter – we might bear in mind that his input could in theory constitute no more than a fifth of the complete work.

Finally, *Ways of Seeing* is made up of seven chapters, but only four of them use words. The others are pictorial essays which present images with no comment and sometimes no identifying caption. By juxtaposing photographs and paintings from diverse moments in culture and history they invite the reader to draw comparisons and contrasts between – to take two consecutive pages from the first picture-essay – an abstract female nude by Picasso, a tall, narrow female in a Giacometti sculpture, a fleshy Rembrandt woman and two pin-ups from 1970s 'girly' magazines. Other sections offer juxtaposed representations of self-portraits, children, death and food within similarly wide ranges. By removing almost all textual information the creators of these essays allow each image to be judged on the same level, without the value-system which prior knowledge might impose, for instance that a Rembrandt must necessarily be 'better' than a soft-porn photograph. However, we should note that as the contemporary examples from magazines and advertisements are given no explanatory credit or source, as opposed to the title, painter, date and nationality carefully listed at the back of the book for every 'work of art', a certain value judgement on the part of the authors is already subtly implied. In some instances, it might be argued further that the distinctions and similarities we are invited to draw are not subtle ones, and make their point quickly rather than prompting debate; given the small-scale, monochrome reproduction of the images on offer, the reader may be inclined to pass through these essays quickly rather than ponder over them in detail. Nevertheless, Berger's declared intention to 'start a process of questioning' through *Ways of Seeing* is already well-served by the form of the book alone; we might well be asking whether a critical argument could not in theory be communicated in pictures as well as, or instead of, words and whether a text like Barthes' *Mythologies* would not make its points more clearly with the addition of a few *Paris-Match* covers for illustration.

The larger part of the book is made up of more conventional, written essays, although these too are liberally illustrated. Broadly speaking, each takes on one major subject related to our 'way of seeing'; that is, questions of how we see, what we see, who is allowed to see, whose view is allowed to become dominant and whose position is served by a particular system of representation.

Art, mystification and ownership

A work of art, Berger proposes early in the first essay, is essentially a record of something seen, a 'relic or text from the past'. As such this kind of image holds the kind of documentary value Raymond Williams spoke about – texts as records of a culture and clues to its structure of feeling – although Berger stresses that he also sees this kind of image as expressive of its creator's personal imagination and experience, rather than as a neutral record.

However, this is not the way our culture tends to view 'works of art.' Our concept of 'art' is loaded with a host of received ideas – 'beauty, truth, genius, civilisation, form, status, taste' – which affect the way we approach art and the way we perceive it. We may feel that, as suggested above, an image 'must' be good because it was created by a recognised 'genius', or 'old master', or even merely because of its form – the use of oil paints, for instance – its presentation or its environment. The circular argument may persuade us that as 'works of art' are hung in a gallery, the images we encounter in a gallery must be works of art. Because of this perception we may be reluctant to criticise or express dislike, or even feel we are unable to comment at all. After all, talking about art is the preserve of 'art critics', who have a specialised vocabulary and uniquely informed judgement.

Berger's project in this first chapter is to expose such perceptions as elitist 'mystification'. That is, they deliberately make art obscure and remote, removing it from the majority and retaining it for a self-selected minority of 'experts'. Berger argues that this process denies us our cultural heritage and our history and, therefore, that it becomes a political issue.

As an example he quotes from a book on the Dutch painter Frans Hals, specifically on the paintings of the Governors and Governesses of an Alms House. The book describes these paintings in vague, abstract terms which almost parody the excesses of 'art appreciation': 'Each woman speaks to us of the human condition with equal importance … subtle modulations of the deep, glowing blacks contribute to the harmonious fusion of the whole and form an unforgettable contrast …'

This is what Berger calls mystification: the use of obscuring language to convince the reader that a painter is somehow giving us insight into the universal, abstract forces of existence. This kind of writing hides the actual historical circumstance of Hals' work, as Berger explains: Hals was a debt-ridden old man at the time of this painting, saved from freezing to death by a hand-out of peat from people just like these.

> The Regents and Regentesses stare at Hals, a destitute old painter who has lost his reputation and lives off public charity; he examines them through the eyes of a pauper who must nevertheless try to be objective ... Hals was the first portraitist to paint the new characters and expressions created by capitalism. (15–16)

The painting is seen to have a specific meaning with a basis in class and historical change, which the 'authority' of the art critic conceals. In theory, Berger argues, this kind of power relation around works of art should no longer be effective. Mass reproduction has meant that anyone could have a poster of 'Regents of the Old Men's Alms House' by Franz Hals on their bedroom wall, watch it broadcast into their living rooms on a television programme or even get the image cheaply transferred onto a T-shirt.

You might recognise at this point that Berger is reworking ideas from Walter Benjamin's essay, 'The Work of Art in the Age of Mechanical Reproduction', which I discussed briefly in the Further Reading for Adorno. But where Benjamin argued that mass reproduction destroyed the 'aura' around the original work of art, Berger believes this aura is still very much intact. Despite, or even because of the multiple reproductions of a work of art, the one in the gallery retains its importance as the 'original', 'enveloped in an atmosphere of entirely bogus religiosity'. Berger imagines a visitor to a gallery, standing in front of the 'original'of a da Vinci painting, and provides the awestruck voice-over: 'I am in front of it. I can see it. This painting by Leonardo is unlike any other in the world. The National Gallery has the real one. If I look at this painting hard enough, I should somehow be able to feel its authenticity ....'

The art work in the gallery has been made into a mysterious, mystifying icon which retains all its old-fashioned value of elitism and minority ownership despite the widespread availability of the image itself. As an alternative, Berger suggests that in place of galleries and museums, the image could be better suited to the office or bedroom pin-board, where it appears in a democratic, mix-and-match assortment of other images, chosen for its relevance to an individual's experience and taste rather than because of a restrictive code of cultural 'value'. This miscellaneous but not arbitrary cut-and-paste gallery of old and new images is, in turn, exactly what we are given by *Ways of Seeing* itself, particularly by the photo-essays.

Women

'Men act and women appear', Berger states at the opening of the second written essay, and from this bold position elaborates a theory of feminine behaviour which he finds supported by a tradition of women in visual representation. A woman, he says, 'born ... into the keeping of men', must constantly watch herself as she acts, knowing that she is the object of others' looks. Through her behaviour she shows others how she wants to be treated, rather than what she wants for herself. 'A woman's presence expresses her own attitude to herself, and defines what can and cannot be done to her ... presence for a woman is so intrinsic to her person that men tend to think of it as an almost physical emanation, a kind of heat or smell or aura.'

This strikes me as mystifying nonsense. In retrospect we can see some of this same tendency towards flights of fancy in the prose – 'when in love, the sight of the beloved has a completeness which no words and no embrace can match ...' – and a distinctly male way of seeing – 'all images are man-made', 'it may be ... that Sheila is one figure among twenty, but for our own reasons she is the one we have eyes for' – in the first chapter as well. It seems strange that given Berger's avowed project to expose dominant mythologies of class and ownership he should at the same time be constructing generalised, vague and patronising explanations of the way women live in contemporary culture. We can only guess that Berger's alternate persona as a novelist tempts him into this romanticised prose and compromises his argument.

There are many valuable observations in his analysis of the female nude through art history, although the distinction he insists upon between 'naked', meaning 'to be oneself' and 'nude' as a form of disguise and display is again arguably over-romantic. Berger shows convincingly that in the Western art tradition, as opposed to other cultural conventions in which naked women are portrayed as jointly involved in sexual activity, female nudes are presented to the viewer as objects to be looked at and admired. To the male owner of the painting this was a form of symbolic possession, emphasising his mastery over the model in particular – for instance, in Charles II's portrait of his mistress – or his masculine command in general, as in the nineteenth-century work by Bouguereau showing a league of some fifty naked nymphs ascending over a pastoral landscape. 'Men of state, of business, discussed under paintings like this. When one of them felt he had been outwitted, he looked up for consolation. What he saw reminded him that he was a man.'

When men appear in the paintings, it is as observers, proxies inside the scene for the male spectator outside the painting; in the Bouguereau, for instance, the foreground is occupied by three appreciative satyrs feasting their eyes on the crowd of naked female bodies. Themes of 'The Judgement of Paris' or 'Susannah and the Elders' similarly became favourites because of the opportunity they provided for naked women being spied on or admired by groups of men. In these and other cases a mirror in one of the models' hands provided the convenient get-out clause that the women represented 'female vanity' and so were virtually asking to be looked at.

Where Berger again allows a subjective romanticism to cloud his argument is in his insistence that there are 'exceptions' to this tradition, in which 'the painter's personal vision of the particular women he is painting is so strong that it makes no allowance for the spectator. The painter's vision binds the woman to him so that they become as inseparable as couples in stone.' This again is itself mystification. However persuasive his arguments may seem that Rubens' portrait of his second wife somehow defies the conventions of the nude and confronts us not as the spectacle of a voyeur but the experience of a lover, Berger fails to recognise that he is only performing the same trick as the 'art appreciation' he derided above: that is, making one individual interpretation appear to be the only obvious meaning.

This refusal to admit any other possible interpretation problematises many of Berger's more sweeping statements in this chapter: in allowing the male observers in paintings to act only as proxies for the male heterosexual viewer, for instance, Berger fails to entertain the possible pleasures of a gay male or heterosexual female in the representations of the men's bodies which are, like the women, almost invariably naked and built along the impressive lines of classical deities. Despite his critique of dominant orthodoxies, Berger seems reluctant in this instance to envisage alternative ways of seeing.

Publicity

Publicity is what Berger calls advertising, and even in the early 1970s it had clearly saturated the urban consciousness. In its tactility, immediacy and its skill at conveying the pleasures of possession, Berger compares the colour photography of advertising – made available only 'fifteen years ago' – to the earlier form of the oil painting. But while the oil painting, whether of a mistress, a platter of food or a prize cow, had been a sign of current ownership, a souvenir of the present, advertising is all about possible possession, deferred possession, possession some time in the future.

The way it works, then, is through a promise that we can become more than we are. We can transform, become richer, even though we of course lose out financially through our purchase of the product.

> Publicity persuades us of such a transformation by showing us people who have apparently been transformed and are, as a result, enviable. The state of being envied is what constitutes glamour. And publicity is the process of manufacturing glamour. (131)

Berger offers us examples from the glossy magazines of the early 1970s, more blatant and unashamed than any we could find today. Men gaze haughtily out at the viewer from the 'exclusive club' they entered when they bought a 'Skopes' suit, 'ready-to-wear and costly ... from just under forty pounds to just over fifty'; another man, smug with the 'different kind of spending power' afforded by Barclaycard, looks knowingly at us as a blonde and brunette cuddle up on each arm. These images, Berger argues, work on envy; envy of ourselves as we could be if we bought the product. As with the oil painting, we imagine ourselves in the picture.

> The spectator-buyer ... is meant to imagine herself transformed by the product into an object of envy for others, an envy which will then justify her loving herself. One could put this another way: the publicity image steals her love of herself as she is, and offers it back to her for the price of the product. (134)

So as well as promoting envy for the self-we-could-be, the advertising image must provoke dissatisfaction with the self-we-are; make us feel insecure, inadequate. Some of the examples Berger gives do this explicitly, playing on fears of bankruptcy. Even today, advertisements aimed at teenagers still tap into fears of having bad skin, of being excluded because of body odour or unfashionable clothes; those for older consumers work the same tricks more subtly, implying through their images the 'enviable' or 'ideal' and encouraging the viewer to judge their own lifestyle, car, body, hair condition and find it wanting.

For this approach to work, Berger argues, requires a certain kind of society; one in which working conditions, inequalities of pay and social powerlessness coax the consumer into feeling unhappy with their way of life but unable to make any fundamental change. Advertising offers the possibility of change; purchasing provides it, but like a brief, temporary drug buzz it only leaves the consumer back where they started, a little poorer and just as unsatisfied. In this way, Berger proposes, consumption takes the place of genuine democracy. In choosing one brand over another – taking the Pepsi Challenge, swapping to Daz, trying new Holsten Pils – we fool ourselves that we are exercising a significant political choice. Some advertising makes this connection explicit by appropriating icons of revolution – 'Join the Freedom-Lovers', says a poster for Berlei bras – to imply that purchase is a political act. A late 1990s equivalent might be the Benetton hoardings which attempt to equate wearing a certain brand of high-street clothes with a battle against racism or a concern for AIDS victims.

It is almost depressingly easy to think of your own examples to back up this section of Berger's argument. Perhaps more striking still is the realisation that this theory is essentially Adorno's, reconstructed some forty years on and without the extenuating context of a Nazi Germany or a highly standardised United States to explain away the more gloomy pronouncements.

Ultimately, though, Berger's project ends with hope, and a trust both in the potential of this popular, accessible programme of education called 'Ways of Seeing' and in the intelligence of its audience. The final words of the book are 'To be continued by the reader ...' The final image is a Magritte, titled 'On the Threshold of Liberty'.

Problems with Berger

On the whole, Berger and his team are creating their own myths here: only one view or interpetation is the 'right' one, and it is presented as if it should be 'obvious'. For instance, asking whether advertising is related to oil painting, Berger asserts 'it is one of those questions which simply needs to be asked for the answer to become clear.' Some might well argue that there should be no such questions; after all, as Barthes has proposed, it is when something pretends to 'go without saying' that it has the most to hide.

Although Berger notes early on that there is such a thing as 'pseudo-Marxist mystification' it is doubtful that he realises some of his own writing could fall into that category, as when he explains that the only alternative to existing within the cycle of envy, purchase and dissatisfaction provoked by advertising is to 'join the political struggle for a full democracy which entails, among other things, the overthrow of capitalism'. This kind of rhetoric, in which the reader is either forced to share the author's political stance or be seen as a hopeless dupe, is reminiscent of nothing so much as F.R. Leavis' bullying method of 'educational' questioning in *Culture and Environment*.

Further reading

John Berger's oeuvre of novels, theory and art criticism includes *A Painter of Our Time* (Secker and Warburg, 1958), *Permanent Red* (Methuen, 1960), *The Foot of Clive* (Penguin, 1962), *Corker's Freedom* (Methuen, 1964), *The Success and Failure of Picasso* (Penguin, 1965), *A Fortunate Man* (with Jean Mohr) (Allen Lane, 1967), *Art and Revolution* (Weidenfeld and Nicolson, 1969), *The Moment of Cubism and Other Essays* (Weidenfeld and Nicolson, 1969), *Ways of Seeing* (Penguin, 1972), *G* (Weidenfeld and Nicolson, 1972), *The Look of Things* (Penguin, 1972), *A Seventh Man* (with Jean Mohr) (Penguin, 1975), *Pig Earth* (Writers and Readers, 1979), *About Looking* (Writers and Readers, 1980), *Another Way of Telling* (with Jean Mohr) (Writers and Readers, 1984), *And Our Faces, My Heart, Brief as Photos* (Writers and Readers 1984) and *The White Bird* (Chatto, 1985).

His most recent work is the fiction trilogy *Into Their Labours*, the novel *To the Wedding* and the book of recollections, *Photocopies* (1996).

Judith Williamson's *Decoding Advertisements* (Marion Boyars, 1978) and Erving Goffman's *Gender Advertisements* (Macmillan, 1979) are both interesting additions to Berger's study of 'publicity' in the 1970s; both refer explicitly to both *Ways of Seeing* and *Mythologies*.

Berger's chapter on women finds intriguing parallels in the essay 'Visual Pleasure and Narrative Cinema' by Laura Mulvey, which is still much-cited in film studies despite a certain clumsiness and over-dependence on Freudian psychoanalysis. First published in the journal *Screen* in 1975, it is now available in *The Sexual Subject* (Routledge, 1992) and worth looking at as an argument along very similar lines to Berger's.

If you like *Ways of Seeing*'s photo-essays you will enjoy Marshall McLuhan's *The Medium Is The Message*, first published in 1967 and reissued by Hardwired in 1997. For this link I am indebted to Geoff Dyer's excellent *Ways of Telling: The Work of John Berger* (Pluto Press, 1986), which remains one of the very few texts on Berger's life and writings.

Links in this book

Berger seems to be following a line somewhere between Benjamin and Adorno; that is, he applauds the mass reproduction of works of art in terms of its power to liberate the image from elitist galleries, but deplores the reproduction of art works in mass 'publicity' which create and satisfy false needs. Overall the technological potential of mass reproduction is treated as neutral, and only its possible uses are judged as democratic – anyone can make their own use of a Franz Hals – or oppressive – a Franz Hals can be used to encourage insecurity in consumers which can only be assuaged through purchase. Rather than an inconsistent wavering between two positions, we could see Berger's argument as occupying a reasonable middle position.

There are clear similarities in subject matter and theme between *Ways of Seeing* and *Mythologies*, despite one's primary concern with British culture of the late 1960s and the other's with French culture of a decade earlier. Barthes and Berger are both interested in the power of magazine and advertisement photography to communicate an ideological message – whether French imperialism or the 'glamour' of a certain product – and both expose these received meanings as 'myths' serving the interests of a specific social class. Many of Berger's examples from advertising, with the 'absent, unfocused look of so many glamour images' would equally fit Barthes' description of myth's 'frozen', 'numbed' quality, while Berger's account of the hopeless aspirations which advertising promotes in the powerless consumer strongly echoes Barthes' observations on the typist who daydreams of attending the posh society wedding, or the working-class readers who fantasise over the unattainably elegant cuisine featured in *Elle*.

It is worth noting that some of Berger's conclusions about the elite nature of the art gallery are drawn directly from the studies of Pierre Bourdieu, whose account of the clothes, food, houses and cars associated with the 'tastes' of upper- and lower-class strata is strongly paralleled in Berger's chapter on publicity's culture of glamour and envy.

Meanwhile, John Hartley's *The Politics of Pictures* and *Popular Reality* in some ways extend Berger's project with short visual essays and analyses of the representation of women, artworks and nationality in the magazines and advertisements of the 1990s.

4 | BIRMINGHAM AND BEYOND

Origins: Stuart Hall and the CCCS

Stuart Hall

Stuart Hall grew up in the 1930s as, in his own words, the blackest member of a middle-class Jamaican family. From an early age Hall rejected the assimilation into white English culture advocated by his father, who had worked his way up through the United Fruit Company and was, in Hall's view, patronised and humiliated by his white colleagues. Spending three years in the sixth form, Hall read Joyce, Lenin, Marx and Freud in addition to works on slavery and black culture and became increasingly determined to leave the country as a result of his political awareness. He gained a scholarship to Oxford and sailed to England in 1951.

During his undergraduate years Hall belonged to a mainly West Indian circle of students, but after winning a second scholarship for postgraduate study in 1954 he began to associate with members of the Communist Party and the Labour Club, engaging in debate on the future of the Left. Among the influences on his own thinking during this period were *The Uses of Literacy, Culture and Society* and the work of F.R. Leavis. Following the British invasion of Suez in 1956 Hall aligned himself with the emerging New Left, a group opposed to both Stalinism and British imperialism, and from this impulse began to edit the journal *Universities and Left Review*. In 1957 Hall moved to London to teach in secondary schools around Brixton and the Oval, travelling to central London in the evenings to work on the journal. As a regular contributor to the *Review*, Raymond Williams was still a major influence.

In 1961 Hall left the *Review*, exhausted by his editorial duties, and took a post teaching what was then called 'complementary' studies – a very early instance of a film and mass media course – at Chelsea College in London. It was during his time at Chelsea that Hall engineered the first meeting between Richard Hoggart and Raymond Williams and completed his first major work, *The Popular Arts*, with Paddy Whannel.

In 1964 Hoggart asked Hall to join him at Birmingham to serve as his deputy at the proposed Centre for Contemporary Cultural Studies. Hall moved once more, followed by his partner Catherine, who had transferred her own studies from Sussex. They were married by the end of the year.

The Birmingham Centre for Contemporary Cultural Studies

Richard Hoggart was director of the Centre from 1964 until 1968, at which point he began his work for UNESCO. Hall was, nominally, the acting director for the next four years until it was accepted that Hoggart was not coming back and Hall became outright head. He led the Centre until 1979, when he was himself succeeded by Richard Johnson; leadership passed subsequently to Jorge Lorrain, and the Centre underwent significant changes as it was renamed a Department of Cultural Studies and began to offer undergraduate programmes for the first time.

During the Hoggart-Hall period, graduate work was shaped by a variety of overarching theories, which emerged in the regular CCCS journal *Working Papers in Cultural Studies*. Hoggart's penchant for studies of everyday, 'lived' culture such as he had carried out himself in *The Uses of Literacy* remained an important trend within the Centre, but under Hall there was a shift away from what was seen as the 'old school' of left-Leavism towards a harder European Marxism. Cultural studies at Birmingham began to draw strongly on sociology, employing detailed ethnographic research of audiences and social groups. Writers entered the communities they were studying and examined actual language, fashion and behavioural codes rather than merely constructing a portrait of society from a distance, as Hoggart had, and engaged with contemporary 'subcultures' of the kind Hoggart had dismissed in his notorious descriptions of modern milk-bar youth. Finally, the Centre encouraged feminism's entry into cultural studies and the analysis of female social groups for the first time; a crucial development but one which viewed even Hall as the 'old guard'.

What follows is a brief account of the major theoretical ideas which governed research at Birmingham during the late 1960s and 1970s.

Hegemony

Hall's model of culture was far closer to that of Berger than to Hoggart's, which had primarily been concerned with small-scale communities. Hall's brand of Marxism, like Berger's, saw culture as a massive apparatus for the subordination of the powerless by the dominant classes. Specifically, Hall drew on and popularised the concept of 'hegemony'. The term was originally associated with Antonio Gramsci, an Italian Marxist of the 1920s and 1930s, to account for the success and popularity of Mussolini's fascism despite its oppression of most Italian citizens. Hegemony implies a structure of invisible, 'naturalised' domination which is not even seen as such by the oppressed; rather than forcing itself on the individuals of a society, it controls them subtly through education and government to the extent that they consent to their own subjection. In Barthes' terms, it demonstrates the power of myth to make social imbalance seem 'common sense'. Within hegemonic control it is almost impossible to organise a revolt, as the majority of people have been beguiled into accepting the system as it stands and see little to revolt against. What two of Hall's jointly edited projects attempt is to expose and critique the hegemonic order in Britain and furthermore to make visible the small-scale resistances at work in various 'subcultures'. *Policing The Crisis: Mugging, the State and Law and Order* (1978) argues partly that the crime of 'mugging' and the social type of the (usually black) 'mugger' were deliberately constructed and built up – made, in Barthes' sense, into myths – through government campaigns, police statistics and tabloid reports. The 'mugger' provided a convenient scapegoat for the 'moral panic' in Britain during the early 1970s and enabled the dominant hegemony to reassert itself through policies of 'cracking down on muggers'. Similar strategies have since been employed around the figures of the aggressive beggar, the ramraider, joyrider and even the 'squeegee merchant'. Along different lines, *Resistance through Rituals*, originally published as a double issue of *Working Papers* from Summer 1975, explored the multiple forms of small-scale rebellion to be found in the cultures of skinheads, rastas and mods, among other groups.

Polysemy

Hoggart, like Leavis and indeed Adorno, had tended to see modern audiences as 'cultural dupes', mindlessly consuming whatever the industry fed them in a one-way process. Each text had only a single meaning, with no space for interpretation; if a pulp novel was 'bad', that was it, and its 'bad' message would be transferred directly to its teenage reader. Hall moved away from this simplistic model – though in retrospect, it may not look much of a journey – expanding the argument in his influential essay 'Encoding and Decoding in Television Discourse' (1973) that texts are 'encoded' by their producers and 'decoded' by audiences, a process which allows the possibility for alternative meanings and interpretations. This potential for multiple meanings in a text is called 'polysemy' and lies at the heart of many later works such as those of Janice Radway and Henry Jenkins below. In practice, though, Hall believed texts were 'structured in dominance' to the extent that only a limited polysemy was possible; the meanings of, say, a news headline were so strongly loaded that only a 'negotiation' with the intended, or 'preferred' meaning would normally be available to the reader. This model was particularly influential for David Morley's work on *Nationwide*, discussed below.

Subcultures and ethnography

As already mentioned, the young researchers of the CCCS ventured enthusiastically into the cultural spaces at which Hoggart had turned up his nose. Dick Hebdige's work on mods, skins, punks and rastas, Paul Corrigan's exploration into hippy drug experiences and Paul Willis' association with the rebellious gangs at a working-class school were a long way from *The Uses of Literacy* and, even recently, Hoggart was disputing the value of studies of 'motorcycle gangs in Birmingham', as discussed above.

Apart from the shift in subject matter, though, the CCCS researchers attempted to immerse themselves in the culture they were studying, spending a great deal of time with the subjects and painstakingly recording even the most apparently mundane conversations for transcription and analysis. This ethnographic approach, bringing the techniques of sociology to bear on a cultural studies which had previously relied on a textual analysis born of literary criticism, was an important antidote to the distance, whether benevolent or critical, which had characterised the discipline since the work of the Leavises.

Feminism

One crucial result of this attention to subcultures was the ethnographic research into the largely-overlooked cultural lives of women and the textual analysis of 'feminine' forms such as the teenage and women's magazine by researchers such as Angela McRobbie, Jenny Garber and Janice Winship. According to Hall, the first major work of the Centre was made up of several papers on women's magazine fiction and was ready to be published in book form when it was unaccountably lost. No photocopies had been made, and the work was never recovered. Hall, subsequently, made a deliberate attempt to invite feminists to the Centre and was taken aback by the result; despite his declared support for feminism, he was seen as a senior figure of patriarchy by the young female students and constantly attacked on matters of principle. Eventually it was the difficulty of being placed in such a position which encouraged him to leave the Centre and join the British distance-learning institution, the Open University, in 1979.

And beyond

While at the Centre, students were encouraged to publish extensively and, while this led to the postponement of many dissertations and a dearth of completed doctoral research projects, many of the most respected and influential names in contemporary cultural studies have their postgraduate roots in Birmingham. I have selected three whose work I regard as representing a particular strand, and listed others in the Further Reading sections.

It will be understood that the convention for giving authors' biographies necessarily changes in the following sections: while Dick Hebdige, David Morley and Angela McRobbie are prominent figures, they have not entered the realm of cultural studies legend which warrants giving their date of birth and an account of their early years.

Further reading

Hall's output of joint-authored and edited work has been prolific, but to date there remains no one accessible volume of his own writing; hence the general discussion of Hall and the CCCS in this chapter in place of closer analysis of a single text. *Policing the Crisis* gives a good idea of Hall's approach, but is a forbiddingly long and dense book; 'Encoding and Decoding' has been reprinted in edited form in anthologies, including Simon During's *The Cultural Studies Reader*. Hall is the author of multiple articles and essays, as listed in the excellent bibliography of *Stuart Hall: Critical Dialogues in Cultural Studies*, detailed below.

Stuart Hall: Critical Dialogues in Cultural Studies, edited by David Morley and Kuan-Hsing Chen (Routledge, 1996) is an indispensable source for further study of Hall; it includes interviews with and essays by Hall in addition to articles about his work by a variety of scholars whose lives he intersected, including Dick Hebdige, Angela McRobbie and John Fiske.

Links in this book

Most obviously, Hall's work evolves from and to an extent reacts against the precedents set by Hoggart and Williams. I indicated in the discussion of hegemony that Hall's view of contemporary culture can be related across to those of Berger and Barthes; it could also be noted that the specific notion of 'criminal types' from *Policing the Crisis* and the general model of a society raised through education and popular culture to accept its subtle domination have much in common with the theories of Michel Foucault.

Styles of resistance: Dick Hebdige

Subculture: The Meaning of Style (1979)

Culture

Like the good postgraduate dissertation in which it undoubtedly has its roots, *Subculture* begins with an account of the proposed method and a round-up of previous theory before getting on with the more enjoyable business of inventorising punk fashions. Hebdige's first chapter would actually be a very useful *Teach Yourself Cultural Studies (1868–1979)* if none other were available: it tours the varying models of 'culture' from Matthew Arnold's – a standard of aesthetic excellence, 'the best that has been thought and said' – to Raymond Williams' – 'culture is ordinary', the study of everyday life – and draws from them a dichotomy around 'cultural value' which he argues informed British cultural studies in its early years, and is certainly evident in Williams' own falling-back on arbitrary distinctions between 'good' football and 'bad' Sunday strip-papers.

Moving sideways to bring in Barthes' *Mythologies*, Hebdige proposes that the influence of semiology and Marxism on cultural studies made the work of Hoggart and Williams seem parochial, the pursuit of 'gentlemen amateurs'. He follows Barthes' theory that all culture is subject to a systematic ideological distortion, 'naturalised' and disguised as myth, into Hall's view of hegemony and of the dominant social interest beguilingly made to seem 'common sense'. This is where Hebdige comes in, employing a semiological analysis – treating the decorations, styles and adornments of subgroups as 'signs' to be decoded – in the examination of counter-hegemonic resistance and subversion.

It gets easier.

Bricolage and Appropriation

Hebdige is particularly, even peculiarly fond of quoting the writer Jean Genet alongside Barthes and Hall. Early on, he remarks on the outrage of the arresting police when they found a tube of Vaseline in Genet's possession, their shock and contempt compounded by the writer's subversion of an everyday object into a gay sex aid. It is this borrowing of a familiar item and the inversion of its normal meaning which Hebdige calls 'appropriation', one of subculture's most potent weapons. Closely linked to the notion of 'bricolage' – which, roughly, translates as an improvisatory 'sticking-together' – it had its most visible form in the punk movement which surfaced during Britain's 'long hot summer' of 1976. 'Literally safety-pinned together', as Hebdige describes it,

> Punk reproduced the entire sartorial history of post-war working-class youth cultures in 'cut up' form, combining elements which had originally belonged to completely different epochs. There was a chaos of quiffs and leather jackets, brothel creepers and winkle pickers, plimsolls and paka macs, moddy crops and skinhead strides, drainpipes and vivid socks, bum freezers and bovver boots – all kept 'in place' and 'out of time' by the spectacular adhesives: the safety pins and plastic clothes pegs, the bondage straps and bits of string which attracted so much horrified and fascinated attention. (27)

As with Genet's Vaseline, the punks' safety-pin aesthetic stole an object from its 'acceptable' context and, sticking it through the nose of the body politic, performed a resonant act of subversion. The punker and his or her adornments – bleached or garishly dyed hair, bin-liner shirts, toilet-chain necklaces – was a walking statement of 'abnormality' and defiance.

The most blatant of late-1970s subcultures, it was not the only one to practise appropriation: the teds stole and transformed a swish, Edwardian gentlemen's style, while the mods cut and tailored Union flags into smart jackets, used pills not as the intended 'cure' but for the buzz they gave along the way and filed metal combs to razor sharpness. Style became a weapon in what Hebdige calls a 'semiotic guerrilla warfare.'

Negotiation

Of course, though, these subgroups were not operating outside 'mainstream' culture; nor were they merely reacting against it. As the very concept of appropriation implies, subcultures work within the system, reliant on a 'dominant' for their borrowing and for a shocked audience to their more audacious inversions. Hebdige reveals a more subtle relation between dominant and subculture than is often imagined; a process not just of reaction but of 'negotiation'. The punk, ted, mod, rasta or skinhead performance is to an extent a stylised dramatisation of cultural concerns and themes at a specific moment; a passion play enacted by mainly working-class youth, it turns back on society some of the signs of its time. Taking, again, the most obvious manifestation,

> the punks appropriated the rhetoric of crisis which had filled the airwaves and the editorials throughout the period and translated it into tangible (and visible) terms. In the gloomy, apocalyptic ambience of the late 1970s with massive unemployment, with the ominous violence of the Notting Hill Carnival ... it was fitting that the punks should present themselves as 'degenerates'; as signs of the highly publicized decay which perfectly represented the atrophied condition of Great Britain. (87)

Similarly, while the sci-fi glam of pop star David Bowie's followers appeared to decline any engagement with class politics, unlike the skinheads and mods, and avoid the territories of racial identity patrolled by teds and rastas, their aesthetic of glittering androgyny both challenged contemporary notions of working-class puritanism and drew on styles made popular by *Cosmopolitan*, nostalgia television and the science fiction blockbuster, amalgamating 'dominant' fashions and visual experiences into a mode of gendered 'otherness'.

Incorporation

Old punks never die; they just end up on 'Welcome to London' postcards sold to tourists on Oxford Street and Charing Cross Road. As Barthes, Berger and Hall had all warned independently, the dominant hegemony is at its most adept when shifting ground to accommodate and deal with a threat to its order: the French Algerian immigrant frozen into a myth of imperiality, the revolutionaries transformed into a Berlei underwear advertisement, the West Indian teenager categorised as a mugger. Hegemony, the strategy of cunning rather than force, of hiding traces rather than highlighting conflicts, has a number of ways to nullify a subversive element quickly and cleanly. Categorising and labelling is one; it is the method Michel Foucault describes for isolating homosexuals, hysterics and criminals alike as pathological 'deviants', and it extends to more contemporary examples such as Hall's mugger and, as Hebdige shows, the football hooligan: 'these people aren't human'.

A more subtle and insidious tactic, though, is simply to absorb the threat into the mainstream, making it acceptable, domestic, trivial. The United States and Britain saw this in the late 1980s with the urban black form of rap music, which was soon made safe for the likes of pretty, white artists such as Vanilla Ice and even Duran Duran; again, in the mid-1990s, drum-and-bass was transformed into a staple of television car advertisements only two years after its birth in British underground dance culture. In 1977 this was the trick played on punk, as British tabloids like the *News of the World* and the *People* ran articles on punk babies, punk brothers and punk-ted weddings until even the cosy, recipes-and-knitting magazine *Woman's Own* could take the subculture under its wing:

> Photographs depicting punks with smiling mothers, reclining next to the family pool, playing with the family dog, were placed above a text which dwelt on the ordinariness of individual punks: 'It's not as rocky horror as it appears'… 'punk can be a family affair' … 'punks as it happens are non-political', and, most insidiously, albeit accurately, 'Johnny Rotten is as big a household name as Hughie Green.' (98)

Myth was already well on its way to doing what it does best, reducing 'a subculture engendered by history, a product of real historical contradictions' to the story of a few talented, nonconformist individuals who made it big; a familiar, frozen portrait of Sid Vicious flicking the Vs and a song about anarchy which, heading the *Best Punk Album in the World...Ever!* now sounds nostalgic, melodic, even strangely quaint.

The Outsider

Hebdige concludes his analysis with another of his idiosyncratic tours around diverse cultural commentators, this time all linked by their position of often self-imposed exile: T.S. Eliot, alienated from 'the vulgar inroads of mass culture: the trashy films, the comics, the mean emotions and petty lives …', Jean Genet, the subversive invert distanced from society by both his criminal sexuality and his finicky tastes and, finally, Barthes in the passage which closes *Mythologies*: 'everything from our theatre, and a murder trial, to the cooking we dream of is cursed, enmeshed for Barthes in a pernicious ideology. Everything nourishing is spoiled; every spontaneous event or emotion a potential prey to myth.'

It is this last position which seems to mirror most closely that of Hebdige: for merely by writing *Subculture*, by attempting to give the 'subordinate' a voice in academia, he has alienated himself from them.

> It is highly unlikely ... that the members of any of the subcultures described in this book would recognise themselves reflected here. They are still less likely to welcome any efforts on our part to understand them. After all, we, the sociologists and interested straights, threaten to kill with kindness the forms which we seek to elucidate. (139)

The theorist of cultural studies, like the mythologist, seems doomed to become 'marginal ... in society but not inside it, producing analyses of popular culture which are themselves anything but popular.' It is an honest and melancholy conclusion, but perhaps an overly gloomy one: there were reports in the 1980s, contrary to Hebdige's prediction, of wannabe mods sharing round a copy of *Subculture*, using its detailed account of requisite mod style as a blueprint, guideline and shopping list.

Problems with Hebdige

While Hebdige is usually admirably precise in his listing of sartorial accessories, obscure Southend bands and newspaper stories sourced to the day of publication, his style goes into apocalyptic overdrive when it comes to describing social conditions or historical circumstances, and so sacrifices authority for effect: punks were 'bound to a Britain which had no foreseeable future', celebrating 'the death of the community and the collapse of traditional forms of meaning'. In turn, America is evoked as 'a fantasy continent of Westerns and gangsters, luxury, glamour and "automobiles",' and Soho as a world of 'dimly lit coffee bars'. Hebdige is reproducing a strikingly Hoggartian myth in these latter passages, without a word of critique, and his ties to the older traditions of cultural studies seem also to remain in his inexcusably snobbish asides about music he doesn't happen to like, such as the 'vacuous disco-bounce and sugary ballads' of pop.

Finally, I have omitted for the sake of clarity here any discussion of Hebdige's attempts to reconcile the psychoanalytic and semiotic theory of Julia Kristeva to subculture, and feel he should have done the same. While

typical of the mix-and-match theory-shopping approach of CCCS cultural
studies – see also McRobbie's inappropriate use of Freudian psychoanalysis
– these passages now seem mystificatory and inconsistent with the main
project.

Further reading

Hebdige is the author of *Cut'n'Mix: Culture, Identity and Caribbean
Music* (Comedia, 1987) and *Hiding In The Light: On Images and Things*
(Routledge, 1988), whose sharp analyses of archetypal 1980s postmodern
culture remain influential.

Subculture's themes of racial and ethnic identity, which constituted an
important strand of research at Birmingham, are taken up more
extensively in the work of Paul Gilroy, who introduces the CCCS joint
volume *The Empire Strikes Back* (1982) and follows it with *There Ain't No
Black in the Union Jack* (Hutchinson, 1987) and *The Black Atlantic*
(Verso, 1993).

Taking an ethnographic approach rather than Hebdige's overview, Paul
Willis' *Learning to Labour* (Saxon House, 1977) and *Profane Culture*
(Routledge, 1978) build, as does *Subculture*, on essays in the *Resistance
Through Rituals* collection. They provide an involving study of diverse
subcultures – schoolboys in the former, bikers and hippies in the latter –
and with hindsight illustrate the pitfalls of this 'participant observer'
method. An additional reason to read Willis alongside Hebdige is that
Angela McRobbie attacks them both as representative of a male-dominated
tradition in her own *Feminism and Youth Culture*, as discussed below.

Lipstick Traces (Secker and Warburg, 1989) and *In The Fascist Bathroom*
(Viking, 1993), both by Greil Marcus, are great books on punk.

Links in this book

The first chapter of *Subculture* could hardly make Hebdige's journey from
Hoggart and Williams through Barthes and Hall more explicit. In terms of
more recent work, *Subculture*'s theories of group-sameness through codes
of difference and small-scale resistance to the 'dominant' find a resonance
in Henry Jenkins' study of science fiction fans, who while more 'straight'
– as in 'uncool' – than Hebdige's punks, rastas and mods, are also
undeniably more 'queer'.

Negotiating the television audience: David Morley

The 'Nationwide' Audience (1980)

A history of audiences

Morley begins his study, much as Hebdige had, with a survey of previous work on audience responses. He outlines the 'pessimistic mass society thesis' of the Frankfurt School and traces the movement of this 'hypodermic' model – so called because the media are seen to 'inject' ideology directly into the consciousness of the masses – to the United States in the 1940s. During the Second World War and immediately afterwards, this model began to be questioned as researchers shifted their attention from the message alone to its effects on the audience. Robert Merton's study 'Mass Persuasion' of 1946, analysing the influence of war bond broadcasts, discovered that certain propaganda techniques worked as effective 'triggers' on an audience while some were unsuccessful; this response depended not just on the nature of the message but on the social context of its reception.

There followed an increased interest in the way a message was received, rather than on the text alone. The 'People's Choice' study of election propaganda (Lazarsfeld and Katz, 1955) proposed that the voter's choice was affected far more by their personal environment and the pressures of their surrounding social group than by media persuasion; propaganda worked in a 'two-step' flow from radio and television broadcasts through 'opinion leaders' – that is, the particularly influential members of any social group, such as a union leader, a dominant grandfather, a well-educated acquaintance – to the rest of the community.

During the late 1950s and 1960s there came to be even more emphasis on the role of the audience, or 'reader' of media texts, in the production of meaning. Far from passively taking in a message 'from above', viewers were often said to actively read their own message from the text; rather than asking what effect the media had on people, the dominant question became 'what do people do to the media?' This model, known as the 'uses and gratifications' theory, remains influential and can be seen at work in much of John Fiske's writing from the 1980s, for instance.

Morley's model

David Morley's position does not precisely coincide with any of these. He sees the 'uses and gratifications' framework as too loose, potentially allowing a text to be read in any way; additionally, it treats society as an 'atomised mass of individuals', devoid of social context and all forming their own unique meanings. To Morley, this is no more accurate or useful than the earlier model of a mass audience all receiving an identical message. What he proposes is that people exist within 'subcultural formations', within social groups or contexts – the school, the workplace, the family – and that these groups 'provide a framework of meaning' within which we form our opinions. Our response to a television programme will be influenced by our position in one of these 'interpretive communities'; and of course these can overlap and subdivide, so that we might be a black graduate who votes Labour, but dislikes Tony Blair, or a female mature student who grew up working-class but has middle-class aspirations, and so be shaped by our membership of several groups at once.

The second plank in Morley's theory is that while a message – for his purposes, a news item on a TV programme – contains more than one potential meaning and is therefore polysemic, this doesn't mean all these meanings are equally available. Polysemy, he argues, is not the same as plurality, and he draws on Stuart Hall's theories of 'encoding' and 'decoding' when stating his central position:

> The TV message is treated as a complex sign, in which a preferred meaning has been inscribed, but which retains the potential, if decoded in a manner different from the way in which it has been encoded, of communicating a different meaning. The message is thus a structured polysemy. It is central to the argument that all meanings do not exist 'equally' in the message: it has been structured in dominance, although its meaning can never be totally fixed or 'closed'. (10)

Morley proposes that the message can be interpreted in three ways: through a 'dominant' reading, where the 'preferred' meaning – that is, the one which the producers intended – is entirely accepted; through a 'negotiated' reading, where aspects of the message are accepted and others rejected, and through an 'oppositional' reading, where the fundamental premise of the message is rejected outright.

The main body of his book is, therefore, an illustration of this model. Twenty-nine audience groups, sized between three and thirteen and selected as representative of various 'interpretive communities' with regard to their age, race, gender, employment, class and political allegiance, were shown two editions of the British television magazine and news programme *Nationwide* taken from 1976 and 1977. The subsequent interviews were taped, transcribed and analysed, except for those where Morley's equipment malfunctioned and the interviews were lost. These little accidents give the research an endearingly flawed and human quality, and also suggest the genuine problems faced by audience research in the 1970s.

Dominant readings

'Dominant', it should be noted, doesn't mean the audience automatically 'naturalises' the ideology of the message and treats it as 'common sense'; the viewer can recognise that the message is biased and from a certain position and still accept it as when, to take a crude example, someone passes a poster warning 'New Labour, New Danger' and thinks 'well, that's obviously Tory propaganda, but yes, they're right.'

In Morley's example, the 'dominant' view is taken by a group of schoolboys, all aged fifteen, half white and half West Indian, in a working-class area of West London. Their attitude to the programme, probably most influenced by their shared age, is what Morley calls a 'deferential' one; rather than questioning the construction or bias of an interview, they feel the interviewer is 'just there doing his job'. Similarly, they endorse the mockery accorded to an item about students wasting taxpayers' money and to the Americans on a Suffolk army base: 'they stick to their own culture and they never changed their way of life', 'they're bigheads and they're lazy'. The schoolboys identify unproblematically with the 'we' proposed by the *Nationwide* presenters – 'we' all know students are wasters, 'we' can laugh at Americans' habits – and have already absorbed certain political ideologies as 'obvious' or 'common sense', as in the comment on strikers that 'there's no point … if they're going to keep striking this country's going to go down and down'.

The other 'dominant' reading group is made up of white, mostly male, bank managers aged from twenty-nine to fifty-two years old and predominantly Conservative voters. As Morley puts it:

> the ideological problematic embedded in the programme provokes
> little comment. It is largely invisible to them because it is so closely

equivalent to their own view ... Indeed, they go so far as to deny the presence of any ideological framework; it's so 'obvious' as to be invisible:

Q: 'What was the implicit framework?'
A: 'I don't think they had one ...'

Oppositional readings

This acceptance of the programme's dominant codes by the bank managers in Group 21 could hardly be more different from Group 22, which consists of male trade union officials aged from twenty-nine to sixty-four and exclusively Labour voting. Asked a similar question about the Budget item's framework, one respondent can hardly contain himself.

> The perspective was that of the poor hard-pressed managerial section ... they had the farm worker there ... that was, sort of, 'well, you've got £1.90 now – are you happy with that – now go away' and then 'Now, you, poor sod, you're on £13,000 p.a ... and a free car ... Christ, they've only given you £1.10 – I bet you're speechless!'

Throughout the broadcast, the union men play to the gallery with a 'spontaneous commentary' and its witty cross-references to the surrounding culture of 1970s Britain are reproduced in meticulous detail: 'Ha! Ha! That's a good one!', 'His lav's bigger than my lounge!', 'Those aren't Marks and Spencer's shoes he's wearing', 'Let's watch *Crossroads* [a 1970s television soap]'. As Morley explains, 'the group find the problematic of the programme quite unacceptable'.

A preference for *Crossroads* is also expressed by one of the other 'oppositional' groups, although this time – the group being made up of West Indian women students who see the programme as 'irrelevant and inaccessible' – their opposition is what Morley describes as 'subcultural' rather than political. These respondents are so alienated by the programme that they cannot discriminate between the items and extend their dislike beyond *Nationwide* to news in general – 'when I stay and listen to the news I fall asleep' – and then to the BBC as a whole: 'I think BBC is boring.' 'BBC is really, really boring ... they should ban one of the stations.'

Negotiated readings

This, the least extreme response, is also the most common, although the motivation behind and the form of the negotiation may vary. Because of this variation in response it is the most difficult to define precisely, but it is typified in Morley's examples by a shifting perspective from one position to another and an uneasy lack of conclusion. In the case of the middle-class white students at a university in Britain's Midlands region, their response to the item on students building a 'Survival Kit' from rubbish materials is initially hostile. The respondents identify the stereotype in use and distance themselves from the 'we' the programme constructs: 'They're living off the state/we pay them grants to do that' is the kind of response that item is asking for. However, this oppositional view is qualified by the students' reminder that 'there is in fact the sort of reality thing behind that – that this is maybe a questionable thing to do with public money ...' Similarly, while they readily see through the 'Americans' items as patronising and built upon stereotypes – 'How typical is that of American life? Essentially atypical. It may be typical of the kind of media image we get of Americans ...' – the stereotype also seems to find some resonance in their own prejudices. 'But there is this thing amongst Americans ... they ask the time, they love the Queen, they come over and stand outside Buckingham Palace ...'

It is this self-contradictory, mobile position that, within Morley's framework, most of us occupy when watching the news, or indeed receiving any text: neither passively taking it in and accepting it as 'obvious', nor actively forcing our own interpretations on the information and disregarding the producer's intention, but engaging in a constant process of negotiation.

Problems with Morley

As Graeme Turner points out in *British Cultural Studies*, Morley himself – in his subsequent book *Family Television* – was among those who offered criticisms of the *Nationwide* project. The various overlapping interpretive communities to which each individual belongs make for a more complex subjectivity than Morley allows in this book – he assumes, for instance, that trade union affiliation will be the dominant factor in determining a reading – and he admits in *Family Television* that the links he attempted to make between the meanings generated and their roots in fundamental class structures were excessively crude.

The conditions of Morley's research are also open to question. Watching a programme with a group of workmates, in an 'academic' situation and in the presence of a researcher, is nothing like sitting in a living room and viewing it alone, or even with your family: Morley does not account for the influence of these significant factors on his groups' response.

Lastly, we might contest Morley's very assertion that texts are 'structured in dominance' and that every reading, even if oppositional, must relate in some way to the meaning 'encoded' in the text. A theorist like Stanley Fish – whose essays are collected in *Is There A Text In This Class?* (Harvard University Press, 1980) – would claim by contrast that a text has no inherent meaning until it is read and is potentially open to an infinite number of interpretations: but some people find such ideas frightening.

Further reading

Of particular note with regard to *The 'Nationwide' Audience* is Morley's earlier work with his long-term partner and collaborator Charlotte Brunsdon, the BFI monograph *Everyday Television: Nationwide* (1978). Comparing the two reveals Morley's own shift from a textual analysis of codes and conventions in the first book to a study of the way those codes are received and modified by audiences in the second. David Morley's later work includes *Family Television* (Comedia, 1986), *Television, Audiences and Cultural Studies* (Routledge, 1992) and, with Kevin Robbins, *Spaces of Identity* (Routledge, 1995).

The project of *The 'Nationwide' Audience* is taken up in a modified form by Dorothy Hobson's *Crossroads: The Drama of a Soap Opera* (Methuen, 1982) and David Buckingham's *Public Secrets: EastEnders and Its Audience* (BFI, 1987).

Links in this book

Morley's examination of the TV audience's role in making meaning has clear links with the work of John Fiske, particularly *Television Culture*. John Hartley's early collaboration with Fiske, *Reading Television* (1978), like the later *Understanding News*, shares Morley's pioneer impulse to take television studies seriously in a period when film studies was very much considered a superior discipline.

Invisible girls: Angela McRobbie

Feminism and Youth Culture (1991)

Boy zone

On a personal level, Angela McRobbie clearly had some affection for her fellow CCCS researchers Dick Hebdige and Paul Willis – Hebdige, she notes in one of many confessional passages, 'was an occasional doorman at the wonderful Shoop disco', while Gilroy 'dj-ed at Digbeth City Hall' – but in terms of her academic project, her first task was to examine their failures and omissions. *Feminism and Youth Culture* is largely made up of this CCCS work, including extracts from McRobbie's MA thesis and her early article from *Resistance Through Rituals*; its explicit purpose is to go beyond what Charlotte Brunsdon – in *Stuart Hall: Critical Dialogues in Cultural Studies* – calls the 'boyzone' of Birmingham research and to make visible the previously marginalised role of young women in popular culture.

McRobbie's criticisms of *Learning to Labour*, Paul Willis' study of working-class 'lads' and their resistance to the authoritarian structures of school life, can hardly be disputed. In his infatuation with the lads' rebellious creativity, Willis neglects to comment on their hostility and contempt towards women, as McRobbie demonstrates through just a few examples:

> One teacher's authority is undermined by her being labelled a 'cunt'. Boredom in the classroom is alleviated by the mimed masturbating of a giant penis and by replacing the teacher's official language with a litany of sexual 'obscenities'. The lads demonstrate their disgust for and fear of menstruation by substituting 'jam rag' for 'towel' at every opportunity. (21)

Willis' admiration for and championing of this 'subversion' becomes increasingly depressing and reaches its nadir at the end of his study, when one of the lads offers the conclusion 'the only thing I'm interested in is fucking as many women as I can if you really want to know.'

While perhaps less obviously problematic, Hebdige's *Subculture* is also singled out for its failure to address issues of gender and the positioning of women within subcultural groupings. Despite their apparent transgressions and inversions,

> the signs and codes subverted and reassembled in the 'semiotic guerilla warfare' conducted through style do not really speak to women at all. The attractions of a subculture – its fluidity, the shifts in the minutiae of its styles, the details of its combative bricolage – are offset by an unchanging and exploitative view of women. (25)

McRobbie suggests that while girls do play a visible, however marginalised part within male subcultures – citing footage of teddy-girls from the 1950s, the girl-mods of the mid-1960s fictionalised in *Quadrophenia* and anecdotal evidence of female skinheads in the 1970s –

they also construct their own distinctive culture centred not on the street but in the home, specifically the bedroom. This more domesticised culture of leisure and consumerism would include the pleasures of experimenting with new clothes and make-up, listening to music and creating styles within a much smaller, more intimate group of close friends. While overlooked by male researchers, these activities have long been recognised and catered for by girls' weekly comics and magazines, with their discourses of fashion, pop and romance.

Girl's world

Before engaging with a textual analysis of these magazines, McRobbie attempts to redress the ethnographical balance through a study of working-class teenage girls at a Birmingham youth club. Her intention here is to question how the girls respond to the various constraints and structures – whether physical, financial, sexual or ideological – on their daily lives, and to what extent they shape their own culture from 'below' this imposed framework. McRobbie's proposed method, making use of various approaches from simple observation through questionnaires and informal discussion to structured interviews, seems laudably straightforward and formalised. In practice, though, an imprecision enters her research from the beginning as she claims that the informal, untaped sessions were by far the most successful, where 'conversations could easily be recorded by note-taking'. As most of the study is made up of quotations, the implication is that we are relying almost entirely on McRobbie's hasty jottings during a group discussion for an accurate record of the girls' views. The authority of the study is further undermined by the fact that McRobbie – in contrast to Willis, who transcribes entire, fairly lengthy conversations – consistently quotes snippets of one sentence or less to support her argument; it is hard not to feel that such brief soundbites could be adapted to prove just about any point.

Aside from its pioneering role in actually investigating the strategies through which young girls structure their leisure, work and school time, this essay is significant in what it reveals about ethnographic research itself and the problems faced by the interviewer. On these issues McRobbie is admirably self-critical, examining the dilemma of the feminist researcher who attempts to engage with subjects on a basis of 'shared feminity' and meets with awkwardness – 'it took a month … before the girls finally stopped calling me "Miss"' – or embarrassed deference – 'why are you interested in me. I'm only a housewife' – and the dangers of either romanticising or patronising the members of the social group under investigation. 'Why should we assume that we can actually do anything for them? How can we assume they need anything done for them in the first place? Or conversely that we have anything real to offer them? What then are the objectives of feminist research?'

While the relentless deliberation and insecurity makes this seem a less sure-footed work of ethnography than *Learning to Labour*, it could readily be argued that male researchers would have benefited from this kind of self-awareness, had they been brave enough to ask such searching questions of their own work.

Jackie

McRobbie has already identified the importance of the 'private sphere' in girls' culture. The British magazine *Jackie*, she argues, enters into this sphere of leisure and free time, offering the teenage girl a structure which subtly prepares her for adult life according to the dominant ideology; that is, encouraging a traditional heterosexual 'femininity' and an appreciation of consumerism. While she makes a point of distancing herself from a Frankfurt-style dismissal of girls' magazines as a medium for creating and satisfying false needs, or conversely a leftist suspicion of such magazines as propaganda designed to keep the working-classes docile and subordinate, McRobbie does not, genuinely, seem to have moved very far from these positions and never entertains the further possibility that *Jackie* may be a site for readers to actively generate – or 'negotiate', as Morley would have it – their own meanings.

For this reason, her analysis tends towards absolutes and assumptions, rather than testing the magazine's effects on the teenage reader. After all her work on ethnography, the neglect on McRobbie's part of any attempt to gauge 'real-life' response – for instance through the kind of interviews which constituted her previous chapter – seems a bizarre omission.

Instead she decides on a semiological analysis, approaching the magazine through various 'codes' which define the different types of article and story. Her subsequent breakdown of *Jackie* features into these categories – the code of romance, of personal/domestic life, of fashion and beauty and of pop music – is, like the ethnographic research above, valuable in its endeavour to try something new, to impose a theoretical framework on the 'trivial' world of girls' magazines for the first time. Again, though, it is characterised by a vagueness and lack of precision. McRobbie's version of semiology doesn't enable her to deal at all adequately, for instance, with the interrelated visual and textual codes of comic strips, which she discusses solely through a description of the story or, once more, through odd snippets of dialogue: 'Hmm, this mightn't be so bad after all ...', 'Hmm, I could enjoy teaching you, love ...', 'Hmm, funny names you call your cats.' We have to trust that McRobbie has taken these weirdly repetitive quotations from a genuine text rather than simply inventing them, as she gives no page numbers, dates or other source for any of her examples.

Just Seventeen

If her weaknesses seem to repeat themselves from chapter to chapter, so do her strengths. McRobbie is happy to criticise and re-evaluate her work and engages in an honest dialogue about her *Jackie* essay as part of the later piece on another British teen-mag, *Just Seventeen*. Her textual analysis, she admits, was far too rigid and prescriptive; subsequent work by other researchers with groups of young girls undermined many of her assumptions and suggested that the magazine was more open to complex readings, contestations and contradictions than she has asserted. 'My own "naive" reading,' McRobbie happily accepts, 'is therefore discredited in favour of a more fluid and ultimately more engaged process of reading in which readers typically participate in the creation of textual reading.'

It is astonishing, then, that McRobbie declines to adapt these approaches into her later analysis. While convincingly arguing that the 'code of romance' which dominated *Jackie* in the 1960s has been replaced by the codes of pop and fashion, leading to the decline of the passive, dependent mode of femininity from the older love stories and an increasingly confident focus on the self, McRobbie's conclusions are drawn entirely from textual evidence – for which she still neglects to provide so much as a page number – rather than from the readers themselves. Her description of the typical *Just Seventeen* reader is blithely sure of itself, from its account of daily lifestyle – 'they will be spending time with each other on Saturday afternoons, hanging about the shopping centres, going to the local cinema ...' – to its identifying of the postmodern, cut up and fragmented aesthetic which informs the young reader's fashion sensibilities. However, as the research she cites above has already demonstrated, it is impossible to 'know' the reader from the magazine alone, or merely to guess the ways in which the text will be received by its audience.

While she constantly refines her ethnographic approach on one hand and her textual analysis on the other, then, the obstacle McRobbie seems unable to overcome is how to combine the two methods into a consistent whole. Because of this, *Feminism and Youth Culture* alternates between 'pure' sociology and 'pure' semiology, between the inspiring and the frustrating, and ultimately refuses to cohere.

Problems with McRobbie

As I have surely made clear, *Feminism and Youth Culture* is an inherently problematic text; however you excuse it and admire it for its first steps in an important direction, it is impossible to ignore McRobbie's apparent failure even in the later essays to learn from what she accepts were her earlier mistakes. Indeed, I have declined to discuss the final two, most recent, chapters in the book because I see them as particularly weak and without a great deal of relevance to the main project: the exclusively textual essay on 'Dance Narratives' and the exclusively sociological conclusion on 'Teenage Mothers' suggest that the inability to combine two modes of approach still haunts McRobbie's work.

On another level, there is a clumsiness and inelegance about McRobbie's style from the first page of this book onwards, characterised by a lazy trailing off into 'etc.' or vague ellipsis. While this may seem trivial, it is symptomatic of the general lack of precision throughout and sometimes spills over into annoying inaccuracies such as the misspellings 'Eastenders' and 'Bladerunner'.

This is in many ways an important collection for what it represents, but it is also desperately, undeniably flawed.

Further reading

McRobbie is co-editor with Mica Nava of *Gender and Generation* (Macmillan, 1984) and author of *Postmodernism and Popular Culture* (Routledge, 1994). Her most recent work to date is *Fashion and the Image Industries*, also published by Routledge.

As noted in the introduction to this section, feminist research constituted a vital and potent subgroup of the CCCS which often critiqued the male-dominated studies of other writers and even alienated the Centre's director. Two other writers emerging from this milieu were Charlotte Brunsdon, who after collaborating with Morley on the first *Nationwide* monograph contributed mainly to others' anthologies until her recent publication of *Feminist Television Criticism* (Routledge, 1996) and Janice Winship, whose *Inside Women's Magazines* (Pandora, 1987) remains an influential study with particular relevance to both McRobbie and John Berger's work on the representation of women.

Links in this book

The work collected in *Feminism and Youth Culture* can perhaps most profitably be compared with Janice Radway's *Reading the Romance*; like McRobbie, Radway examines the codes of popular 'female' texts – although her audience research is far more rigorous than McRobbie's on *Just Seventeen* – and struggles to reconcile what she considers the reactionary content of these texts with her own feminism.

5 | THE FRENCH CONNECTION

Despite the growth of cultural studies at Birmingham and around other Centres such as Glasgow, the approaches developed by Hall and his students were not immediately picked up outside Britain. One reason for this is the comparatively parochial, small-scale focus of the studies such as those discussed above; it can readily be imagined that specifically British texts like *Nationwide* and *Just Seventeen*, to say nothing of a local girls' youth centre or motorbike gang, did not command much attention in the universities of Australia or the USA. More generally, the Marxist slant and concern with British class structures evident in much CCCS work held little appeal or relevance for Australian and US academics, who liked to regard their own societies as 'classless'.

It is here that the influence of French theory plays a vital part in the development of cultural studies. In contrast to the CCCS researchers, Michel Foucault, Pierre Bourdieu and Michel de Certeau – while they should in no way be regarded as a unified French 'group' – shared a tendency to see power as dispersed and decentred, rather than administered by a central agency. As the New Right took power in the USA under Ronald Reagan and in Britain under Margaret Thatcher, the latter declaring there was no longer any such thing as 'society', so new models of power, dominance and of resistant strategies emerged in cultural studies. In place of class struggle, the discipline began to focus on a more dispersed 'micropolitics' based around gender, sexuality and ethnicity, which was far more adaptable to other national cultures than the earlier British model. In this sense, while cultural studies was born and spent its teenage years in the UK, it took the intervention of French theory to transform it into a truly international discipline and bring it, if not to maturity, then to a confidently jet-setting young adulthood.

Structures of power: Michel Foucault

Michel Foucault was born in 1926 to a middle-class family in Poitiers, France. His father, a doctor, sent him to a Catholic school and he progressed to the prestigious Ecole Nationale Superieure in Paris, during which time he was briefly a member of the French Communist Party. Foucault received his diploma of philosophy in 1949 but became dissatisfied with the subject and fell back on his other interest, psychopathology; a pursuit which resulted in his first book, *Maladie Mentale et Psychologie* (1954). Foucault taught at the University of Uppsala for four years, and was made Director of the French institutes of Warsaw and Hamburg, where he completed his doctoral thesis on the history of madness.

In 1960 he was appointed head of the philosophy department at the University of Clermont-Ferrand and taught there until the publication and immediate success of *Les Mots et les Choses* in 1966 took him back to Paris. During the late 1960s he taught philosophy at the University of Vincennes in a period of intense and sometimes violent political activity and continued to lecture as the chair of History of Systems of Thought at the College de France. In the 1970s Foucault became increasingly politically active, working through the Group for Information about Prisons for penal reform and speaking openly for the gay movement. In the early 1980s he found a new audience among West Coast audiences of the USA.

Michel Foucault died in 1984 of AIDS-related illnesses.

Discipline and Punish: The Birth of the Prison (1975)

Punishment as spectacle

The basic project of *Discipline and Punish* is to describe a change in method for dealing with criminals. Foucault locates this shift around the time of the Enlightenment with its drive for rationalism and reform; by 1840, he asserts, the changes were complete.

The first penal age Foucault describes is that of the eighteenth century, when punishment was an occasion for mass spectacle and drawn-out rituals of torture. Foucault's opening set-piece is one of the most stomach-churning passages you will encounter in an academic text and vividly brings home the nature of this punishment through the example of Damiens, a regicide who met his death in Paris on 2 March 1757. A short extract will give the flavour:

> ... the executioner, his sleeves rolled up, took the steel pincers,
> which had been especially made for the occasion, and which were
> about a foot and a half long, and pulled first at the calf of the right
> leg, then at the thigh, and from there at the two fleshy parts of the
> right arm; then at the breasts. Though a strong, sturdy fellow, the
> executioner found it so difficult to tear away the pieces of flesh that
> he set about the same spot two or three times, twisting the pincers as
> he did so, and what he took away formed at each part a wound about
> the size of a six-pound crown piece. (4)

Foucault provides four pages in the same vein, elaborating on the precise
nature of Damiens' torture until no reader could remain unconvinced that
the penal system in 1757 was very different from our own. The emphasis
in this earlier system was on the corporal; punishment was articulated
through the body. The criminal had addressed an insult to the sovereign's
'body' – that is, the body politic or state, except in extreme cases of
attempted assassination or actual regicide – and the sovereign responded
through an excess of force brought to bear on the body of the criminal.
Hence, in Damien's case, the 'unnecessary' series of mutilations involving
flesh torn away with pincers, burning with sulphur, the application of
molten lead to the wounds, drawing and quartering by four horses and
finally the destruction of the corpse by fire. The state reaffirmed its control
through a display of absolute power over the body, made public as a
warning and deterrent.

Paradoxically, though, the spectacle of punishment, rather than producing
a cowed and respectful citizenry, became an occasion for carnival and an
overturning of conventions. The executioner was rounded on for his
cruelty; rioters were freed by their fellow protestors; the crowd cheered
the blasphemies and oaths of the condemned man, who in his agonies was
in a unique position to break taboos and voice forbidden sentiments. Even
within its own terms – that is, if we accept torture as an entirely
appropriate response to crimes against the state – the earlier penal system
embodied problematic contradictions.

A mere eighty years after the death of Damiens, things had already changed
dramatically. A new system was in place which would lead to a 'sobriety'
of execution, carried out through precise hanging machines or guillotines
and eventually performed only in secret. In place of the executioner, an
'army of technicians ... warders, doctors, chaplains, psychiatrists,
psychologists, educationalists' took on the job of dealing with the prisoner,

with the intention not of torturing but of curing, rehabilitating, correcting and reclaiming the individual. Punishment was no longer carried out on the criminal's body to demonstrate the furious strength of the state; instead it focused on the 'soul' of the wrongdoer. This shift in emphasis involved an entirely different set of questions on the part of the penal system. Previously, it had only been necessary to ascertain whether a crime had been committed and who was responsible, a process which was carried out in secret and often in the absence of the accused; confession under torture would 'prove' guilt. Now the issues were far more complicated:

> It is no longer simply: 'Who committed it?' But 'How can we assign the causal process that produced it? Where did it originate in the author himself? Instinct, unconscious, environment, heredity?' It is no longer simply: 'What law punishes this offence?' But: 'What would be the most appropriate measures to take? How do we see the future development of the offender? What would be the best way of rehabilitating him?' (19)

As Foucault concludes, 'Punishment had gradually ceased to be a spectacle ... from being an art of unbearable sensations punishment has become an economy of suspended rights.' And for this new system, a new apparatus was necessary: not the public scaffold but the panopticon.

Surveillance and the panopticon

In one important respect, *Discipline and Punish* – like *The Practice of Everyday Life* below – fails to communicate the exact sense of Foucault's original title, *Surveiller et Punir*. As other commentators have pointed out, the German *Uberwachen und Strafen* does it more successfully; but in English, 'Survey and Punish', 'Watch Over and Punish' or any conceivable variant such as 'Inspect or Observe' – would seem awkward. Apparently it was Foucault himself who suggested 'discipline' as the closest equivalent. As such, the notion of 'surveillance' is never foregrounded in the English, though it remains the central idea of Foucault's thesis.

In the new penal system, a crucial shift was that the means of policing, previously a cause for spectacle, became invisible. The state exnominated itself, disguised itself as 'neutral' and retreated into the background, but in so doing became if anything more powerful than before, penetrating every area of society and yet apparently coming from nowhere. In turn, the individual – in the first place the criminal, but as we shall see, by no means exclusively so – was made visible; quantified, classified and above all 'observed'. The supreme metaphor for this new system is a form of prison-building designed by Jeremy Bentham, called the Panopticon.

> We know the principle on which it was based: at the periphery, an annular building; at the centre, a tower; this tower is pierced with wide windows that open onto the inner side of the ring; the peripheric building is divided into cells, each of which extends the whole width of the building; they have two windows, one on the inside, corresponding to the windows of the tower; the other, on the outside, allows the light to cross the cell from one end to the other. All that is needed, then, is to place a supervisor in a central tower and to shut up in each cell a madman, a patient, a condemned man, a worker or a schoolboy. By the effect of backlighting, one can observe from the tower, standing out precisely against the light, the small captive shadows in the cells of the periphery. They are like so many cages, so many small theatres, in which each actor is alone, perfectly individualised and constantly visible. (200)

We have come, then, from the display of state punishment to the invisible observer; from the theatre of public torture to the 'small theatre' of the private cell; from the 'art of unbearable sensation' to the 'economy of suspended rights'. Of all these suspended rights, for the prisoner of the Panopticon the most crucial is the loss of privacy, of liberty, of invisibility.

The carceral society

Yet note that the prisoners in Foucault's description are not just criminals; along with the condemned man are placed the insane, the worker, the patient and even the schoolboy. The Panopticon is just a paradigmatic model for the post-Enlightenment society as a whole; that is, the 'panoptic' society or the 'carceral' society, from 'incarceration' or imprisonment. To Foucault, we are all inmates of this system which controls and orders its citizens through subtle, invisible processes of discipline. Workplaces are segregated according to the different roles and status of the occupants – typists in a 'pool', executives in private offices – schools and army barracks alike regulated by timetables as strict as a prison, their rules and schedules controlling dress, movement, speech, even eating and bodily functions while their structure of examinations produces a hierarchy of rank, of 'bright' and 'slow' students. In the background, meanwhile, the health and social security services and the police system in its most literal form builds files on each individual which will follow them from school to school, prison to prison, job to job.

In addition to observing, the network of surveillance categorises and identifies us, labelling and even pathologising those it sees as a danger to the norm. In Foucault's account the key term is the 'delinquent', a 'criminal type' which emerged during the last century, but the process can be applied to anyone considered 'deviant', transforming them into a social enemy and threat to order: we might add to the list the typically female 'hysteric' of the late nineteenth century, the 'Jew' of 1930s Germany, the 'Communist' in McCarthyite America of the 1950s, the 'black mugger' of Stuart Hall's 1970s study and the AIDS-spreading 'homosexual' of the 1980s in particular.

The panoptic system has become our common, 'commonsensical' social structure, regulating itself with only minimal state intervention as citizens police themselves and each other. Foucault, writing in 1975, could not have forseen the rise of closed-circuit television in every city, the demand for 'smart' ID cards or the British government's campaigns encouraging individuals to 'Beat a Cheat' by informing on dole-scrounging neighbours. As 1975 and indeed *Nineteen Eighty-Four* grow increasingly distant, it nevertheless becomes increasingly difficult to dismiss Foucault's claims that we are all potentially being watched at any moment without having any way of knowing or proving it.

Problems with Foucault

J.G. Merquior's *Foucault*, listed under Further Reading below, boldly describes aspects of *Discipline and Punish* as 'shoddy' and 'sloppy'. While this may seem excessively harsh, even the most fervent Foucauldian should take note of certain points Merquior and others – including Michel de Certeau below – have raised against the book. Firstly, Foucault's historical analysis seems over-simplistic, ironing out inconsistencies to fit his theory of a clean transition from one penal system to another; Merquior remarks that he owns a poster from 1813 – that is, from a period Foucault identifies as belonging to the sober 'panoptic' society – detailing the public humiliation and five-year imprisonment of a worker for the mere theft of two handkerchiefs. The traditional penal system had, Merquior suggests, a 'long afterlife' which Foucault chooses to ignore.

Secondly, Foucault gives no account of the way the panoptic system, devised for the specific institution of the prison, infiltrated other spheres of public life such as the school and factory which, unlike prisons, are not cut off from society as a whole. We may be seduced into granting Foucault the extension of his image from the literal Panopticon to a metaphor for society in general, but on closer examination he provides no convincing historical causes or explanations of this process.

Finally, Merquior asks whether the unopposed rise of the carceral system which Foucault describes is not a grossly simplified view of the way a society develops. 'Is not the actual historical record a mixed one, showing real libertarian and equalizing trends beside several configurations of class power and coercive cultural traits?' This is much the line taken by Certeau in his criticism of *Discipline and Punish*. His alternative theory of a constant interplay between imposed control and oppositional response will be discussed at more length below.

Further reading

Les Mots et les Choses was translated as *The Order of Things* (Random House, 1970); *Discipline and Punish*, originally published by Pantheon in 1977, is now available in a Penguin edition. *The History of Sexuality Volume One: An Introduction* and *Volume Three: The Care of the Self* were both reissued by Penguin in 1990 and *The Foucault Reader*, edited by Paul Rabinow (Peregrine, 1986), contains various essays including the influential 'What is an Author?'

J.G. Merquior's *Foucault* (Fontana Modern Masters, 1991) is, as the brief discussion above may have suggested, a particularly wry and irreverent treatment. Others include Simon During's *Foucault and Literature* (Routledge, 1992) and David Macey's *The Lives of Michel Foucault* (Hutchinson, 1993).

Links in this book

Michel de Certeau, as already noted, provides intriguing counter-arguments to much of *Discipline and Punish*. The practice of classifying and pathologising social groups as 'delinquent' or 'deviant' has relevance, as noted above, to the work of Stuart Hall on the figure of the black 'mugger'. Less obviously, Foucault's account of the categorisation and surveillance of 'deviant' sexuality could be related to the discussion in Henry Jenkins' *Textual Poachers* of gay fan-groups and their resistance to the conventions which define homosexuality as an aberration.

Structures of taste: Pierre Bourdieu

Pierre Bourdieu, the son of a civil servant, was born into a petit-bourgeois family on 1 April 1930 and grew up in a small rural town in south-eastern France. In the early 1950s he attended the elite Ecole Normale Superieure in Paris and graduated in Philosophy despite his refusal, in protest at the authoritarian methods of education on offer, to write a thesis. Bourdieu taught in a provincial school for two years before his conscription into national service in 1956; his time in Algeria and guilt at the situation he witnessed there spurred him to write *Sociologie de l'Algerie*, published in 1958. He remained in Algeria, teaching at the University of Algiers and undertaking further sociological research, until 1960.

During the early 1960s Bourdieu worked at the University of Paris and attended lectures by the anthropologist and structuralist Claude Lévi-Strauss which committed him more firmly to a career in social science, rather than the philosophy of his earlier education. By 1964 he was Director of Studies at the Parisian Ecole des Hautes Etudes and four years later founded the Centre of European Sociology, leading research groups and editing the Centre's distinctive journal. Bourdieu's reputation grew rapidly as he continued to publish and, in 1981, he was appointed Chair of Sociology at the College de France.

He continues to hold these positions today.

Distinction: A Social Critique of the Judgement of Taste (1979)

Distinction is based on two surveys carried out by questionnaire in 1963 and 1967–8, on a sample of 1,217 people in Paris, Lille and 'a small provincial town'. The questionnaires, reproduced in an appendix, begin by asking age, gender and occupation – 'be as precise as possible', the text adds, for reasons which will become clear – and go on to interrogate the respondent's preferences in home furnishings, film genres, dinner parties, pieces of music and painters, among other cultural areas. There follows a brief checklist which was filled in by the interviewer in private and describes the subject as he or she came across; 'well groomed or not', 'mistakes in grammar', 'moustache (specify type)' and so on. By the end, the interviewer would have built up a fair picture of the respondent's 'taste': a portrait which, added to all the others and divided into subgroups according to occupation, was used to build up a scheme of lifestyle choices and their relation to class position.

This straightforward project forms the backbone of *Distinction*. It is useful to bear it in mind, as Bourdieu's notoriety for 'difficult' prose is often fully deserved and the accessible visual style of the book, with its tables, newspaper extracts and photographs, is in many ways deceptive. Rather than delving into the mass of observations and statistics, I feel it is wiser here to draw out the key ideas of Bourdieu's theory and link them where possible to the detail of the study.

Capital

Bourdieu likes to present life as a game. Capital is the currency. Whereas classical Marxism sees capital as purely economic, Bourdieu extends the concept – as Adorno extended the term 'industry' – to include the cultural. Economic capital, in his scheme, is still central to social power and in turn to the enforcing of class divisions; but the separate currency of cultural capital also has an important role to play. An 'agent', or player in the game, may possess both, or one, or neither, and the complex interplay of these two forces – which can of course fluctuate, for instance with a sudden redundancy or enrolment on a degree course – determines the agent's 'life chances'. Put simply, capital is the hand you are dealt. We could consider economic capital as hearts and diamonds and cultural capital as spades and clubs; at any stage of play you might hold mainly red or mainly black cards, but they still add up to a set of points. Though you might start with a weak hand – take Richard Hoggart as an example, growing up without parents in an impoverished corner of Leeds – it is possible to play the cards adeptly and gain, say, a scholarship to university and perhaps a post as Professor of English at Birmingham. We can see that cultural and economic capital do often go hand-in-hand, but equally that a player could build one and not the other; there are a lot of postgraduate students on the breadline and many successful entrepreneurs who left school aged fifteen.

Habitus

While Bourdieu's appropriation of the Latin word *habitus* is one of his most important theoretical moves, the concept is a slippery one and Bourdieu refrains from pinning it down with a straight definition. As its root suggests, it involves practices, systems and rules picked up by 'habit', first in the family home – that is, the primary habitus – then modified and built on by the individual's movement through education, work and other social environments into a secondary or tertiary habitus. It constitutes a way of understanding and dealing with the world which we acquire through experience and is, therefore, to an extent unique, but it also relates across to our social position and, most importantly, back to the environment we grew up in.

The primary habitus remains fundamental to our understanding and perception no matter how later experiences transform our economic or cultural capital. Look again at Hoggart, whose working-class habitus marked him as an outsider in higher education, or at Raymond Williams, carrying a childhood in Pandy into the 'high cultural' sphere of Cambridge, or at Stuart Hall, whose Jamaican upbringing and memories of his father followed him to Oxford. However, it can equally be seen that the habitus is not a prison; it determines options to an extent, but allows for the possibility of individual mobility, as the three examples above clearly demonstrate. Finally, as the habitus is constituted of various factors – class, ethnicity, gender, education, status – the habitus of an individual may mesh with a number of collective habituses according to a shared experience of oppression or domination. These patterns can be complex: note that Hall, despite a radically different ethnic background to that of Raymond Williams, nevertheless identified with the Welshman's experience of alienation and colonialism.

In Bourdieu's research, habitus provides a system of classification which enables him to identify specific aesthetic 'lifestyle' choices, or 'tastes', with class positions; through the habitus, the distribution of capital is transformed into recognisable qualities and practices. For instance, on Bourdieu's double-page chart which constellates specific professions with typical preferences, we see around higher education teachers, with high cultural but low economic capital, a taste for chess, *Le Monde*, left-bank galleries, Chinese restaurants and Warhol; on the other side, where private sector executives possess high economic but low cultural capital, the taste is for the Automobile Club, business meals, trade fairs, water-skiing and *Le Figaro*. At the bottom, by contrast, those with a weak hand in both categories favour bread, pasta, potatoes, football and public dances; their lack of economic currency obliges them to eat cheaply, while their low cultural capital means that their appetite for 'art' goes no further than a local kickabout.

Yet crucially, the habitus will have made the individuals in this latter group not just used to but entirely comfortable with this style of living;

their meals and entertainment seem good, honest fare and, rather than aspiring to either Chinese food or auctions, such pursuits will be seen as fancy, pretentious, all right for some but not their cup of tea. *The Uses of Literacy* provides ample examples of this mentality from 1930s working-class England. Bourdieu's account of two very different mealtimes in 1960s France also makes the point vividly. Within the bourgeoisie,

> form is first of all a matter of rhythm, which implies expectations, pauses, restraints; waiting until the last person served has started to eat, taking modest helpings, not appearing over-eager. A strict sequence is observed and all coexistence of dishes which the sequence separates, fish and meat, cheese and dessert, is excluded: for example, before the dessert is served, everything left on the table, even the salt-cellar, is removed, and the crumbs are swept up. (196)

Compare this to the working-class meal,

> characterised by plenty ... and above all by freedom. 'Elastic' and 'abundant' dishes are brought to the table – soups or sauces, pasta or potatoes ... and served with a ladle or spoon, to avoid too much measuring and counting ... to save washing up, the dessert may be handed out on improvised plates torn from the cake-box (with a joke about 'taking the liberty' to mark the transgression) and the neighbour invited in for a meal will also receive his piece of cardboard (offering a plate would exclude him) as a sign of familiarity. (195)

Cultural distinctions – and correspondingly, unequal divisions in capital – are not largely perceived by either upper or lower classes as economically imposed or historically contingent, but, again due to the acquired dispositions of the habitus, as inherited and natural. The habitus, and the system of 'taste' which it defines, therefore works to reinforce and legitimise social separations and social hierarchies, although an individual gaining social mobility and moving through different classes will be in a position to view these structures more clearly and may choose to question them.

Fields

If life is a game and capital the points, then field is the pitch, the board, the court, the terrain. A field is a site of conflict and struggle, a network of relationships within which each agent invests his or her capital and attempts to maximise it. An overarching 'field of power' works as a blueprint for the entire society, determining the fundamental power relations and structures of dominance. We are all born into this field, where those in certain positions are designated 'dominant' and accorded a wealth of economic or cultural capital and those entering the game at another point are subordinate, with correspondingly weak cards to play. However, this vast societal field breaks down into smaller fields, just as the map of a nation subdivides into regions, counties, cities and towns, and within these fields a further complex of power relations comes into play.

While the 'dominant' class of society includes those high in cultural and economic capital, for instance, in practice those working in education or culture are subordinate to those working in business and commerce: economic capital is currently valued more than cultural, as can readily be seen by comparing the salaries of a company's chief executive and the head of a university department. Yet the map breaks down further. Education itself can also be seen as a self-contained field in which groups and individuals jockey for power and prestige. Even a single college, as a complex network of interaction and competition, could be considered a field in its own right. Nevertheless, the fundamental structures of the 'field of power' are echoed in each smaller field; the Oxbridge encountered by Raymond Williams and Stuart Hall was effectively a microcosm of England as a whole and regarded them with suspicion in keeping with national prejudices.

Problems with Bourdieu

According to Bourdieu's gameplan, we are ranked at birth and placed accordingly in either weak or strong positions. From this beginning our primary habitus will tend to resign us to our situation, disguising it as 'natural' rather than contingent and reinforcing class divisions through a system of aesthetic 'taste'. Mobility is possible, but difficult; the three academics I have taken the liberty of using for my examples above were without doubt the exceptions in their communities. There is a certain inevitability and fatalism about this vision of society which does not allow much space for resistance; a point which Michel de Certeau argues below.

Secondly, while the extension of 'capital' to include culture is a significant theoretical move, it has the effect of reducing all culture to a means of emphasising and legitimising systems of domination. There is surely a simplification at work if the art of Buñuel, Kafka, Brecht and Duchamp can be ironed out, as Bourdieu does in the chart cited above, into straightforward signifiers of 'taste' which express a possession of economic capital. Bourdieu is perhaps over-hasty in connecting a liking for these forms of culture to a single, educated middle-class habitus; Bertolt Brecht for one would have been surprised and dismayed to find his plays were only accessible to agents with high economic capital, and evidence suggests that they also played a part alongside the 'bread, potatoes and ordinary red wine' of working-class culture. Culture may sometimes operate as a currency, but it can surely also unsettle and question precisely those class divisions and power relations which, according to Bourdieu, it only serves.

Further reading

Bourdieu's major works comprise *Reproduction in Education and Society* (Sage, 1977), *Outline of a Theory of Practice* (Cambridge University Press, 1977), *Distinction: A Social Critique of the Judgement of Taste* (Routledge, 1984), *Photography: A Middle-Brow Art* (Polity, 1990), *The Love of Art: European Museums and their Public* (Polity, 1990) and *The Field of Cultural Production: Essays on Art and Literature* (Polity, 1993).

Richard Jenkins' *Pierre Bourdieu* (Routledge, 1992) is an intelligent and healthily critical account of Bourdieu's work; while Jenkins does a thorough job of interrogating Bourdieu's ambiguities and inconsistencies, this approach does tend to make the issues more complex rather than immediately accessible. Other commentaries include Craig Calhoun, Edwards LiPuma and Moishe Postone's *Bourdieu: Critical Perspectives* (Polity, 1993) and Derek Robbins' *The Work of Pierre Bourdieu* (Open University Press, 1991).

Links in this book

Michel de Certeau has a fair amount to say about Bourdieu, much of it sceptical, and is the only writer whose work discussed here engages directly with Bourdieu's theories. However, John Berger draws on Bourdieu's sociological account of attitudes towards art galleries in *Ways of Seeing* and both writers, more fundamentally, deal with the role of perceived aesthetic taste – in Berger's case, through notions of 'glamour' and envy – in the maintaining of social divisions.

Living in the gaps: Michel de Certeau

Michel de Certeau was born in Chambery, France, in 1925. Taking degrees in Classics and Philosophy at the universities of Grenoble, Lyon and Paris, he joined the Jesuit order in 1950 and was ordained six years later. During the 1960s, Certeau edited and contributed to French Catholic journals and undertook research into religious history. The protests and social uprising of 1968 prompted him to publish an assessment of the year's events titled *Starting to Speak: Towards a New Culture* and nudged his research interests away from religion towards more varied social and intellectual issues including contemporary politics and Lacanian psychoanalysis. These investigations resulted in the books *Culture in the Plural* (1974) and *The Practice of Everyday Life* (1980). From 1978 to 1984, Certeau held a full-time post in California, and travelled widely while retaining the emotional and intellectual detachment he had inherited from his earlier Jesuit training. He died on 9 January 1986.

The Practice of Everyday Life (1980)

Although I am grouping these three French writers together in one chapter for convenience, and despite the similarities in their view of contemporary society's decentred networks of power, it must be stressed again that this was in no way a 'group' like Frankfurt or Birmingham, and that each was extremely sceptical towards the other's work. In *The Practice of Everyday Life* Certeau takes a whole chapter out from discussion of his own theory to criticise the approach of Foucault and Bourdieu, who in turn had little time for each other. While this critique falls in the book's second section, it seems neater to deal with it first here.

Problems with Bourdieu and Foucault

Certeau wryly describes the theoretical approach he sees in Foucault and Bourdieu as a 'recipe': 'cut out and turn over'. What he means is that both isolate a specific practice from history or anthropology – Foucault's 'panoptic' surveillance, Bourdieu's 'habitus' or strategies of learned behaviour – and subject it to an inversion which makes it seem to explain everything. A single device is being 'cut out' of the whole picture and 'turned over' into an all-encompassing theory. The panopticon allows Foucault's discourse 'to be theoretically panoptical, seeing everything'; Bourdieu's notion of habitus 'is also inverted in order to give its plausibility and its essential articulation to a theory recognising the reproduction of the same order everywhere.' Previously obscure practices are thus singled out and made 'luminous', supposedly able to cast light over society in its totality.

Certeau, questioning this over-simplified picture, cannily asks why the panoptic practice of surveillance became dominant over all others, and what became of the other procedures which were never adopted into the dominant system. If one system rises to the foreground, there must be countless alternatives waiting in the background: 'beneath what one might call the "monotheistic" privilege that panoptic apparatuses have won for themselves, a "polytheism" of scattered practices survives, dominated but not erased by the triumphal success of one of their number.' Society, Certeau is arguing, cannot be reduced to a single model. Rather than one all-encompassing 'organising discourse' such as the panopticon or the habitus, we should envisage a network of both normative institutions – control through surveillance, cultural convention and class disposition – and a host of other, minor, contradictory discourses.

These other discourses are the near-invisible practices which go on in the gaps of the system and out of sight of panoptic surveillance; this is the unconventional behaviour which Bourdieu dismisses as a 'short-term and short sighted', 'anarchical', 'bric-a-brac' response to societal structures. It is these small acts of resistance and creativity which interest Certeau, and he labels them 'tactics'.

Strategies and tactics

So while Foucault describes the mechanisms of power inscribed through invisible surveillance and categorisation onto the fields of education and discipline, Certeau wants to know how people avoid, evade and resist these mechanisms. Not through any kind of organised revolt – although 1968 provided an exception to this rule – but by manipulating in small ways within the system. Indeed, the French title *Arts de faire*, which became *The Practice of Everyday Life*, might have been better translated as 'the art of making do'.

Within systems of dominance, or 'strategies', there are always 'tactics' on the part of the dominated; a culture imposed from above is interpreted, subverted and made use of from below, just as the rules of language – grammar and syntax – are toyed with and twisted in the slang and dialect of spoken conversation, or an indigenous people adapts and improvises the culture forced on them by a colonising nation. What results is, says Certeau, a truly 'popular' culture, manufactured from scraps and bric-a-brac.

'Users make innumerable and infinitesimal transformations of and within the dominant cultural economy in order to adapt it to their own interests and their own rules.' Certeau uses the word '*bricoler*' for 'make' in his original text, which may bring to mind Dick Hebdige's employment of the same term to describe punk's creative inversion of the 'conventional' object into resistant subculture. Within Certeau's theory perhaps we are all punk in our own small way, inventively resisting the rules of school, work, even the law.

Example: *La Perruque*

A friend told me that at about four-thirty, towards the end of his working day, he begins to take longer and longer trips to the company toilets, sometimes spending up to twenty minutes in that solace reading a magazine. I doubt he realised he was practising an art of everyday life, any more than I did when I used to run off fifty issues of a fanzine on my department's photocopier; but these are both perfect examples of what Certeau calls '*la perruque*'. Literally 'the wig', *la perruque* is the ability to do your own work, or enjoy your own pleasures, on company time. As opposed to pilfering, *la perruque* doesn't imply material theft; it is 'a secretary's writing a love letter ... a cabinetmaker's "borrowing" a lathe to make a piece of furniture for his living room.'

> The worker who indulges in *la perruque* actually diverts time (not goods, since he uses only scraps) from the factory for work that is free, creative, and precisely not directed toward profit. In the very place where the machine he must serve reigns supreme, he cunningly takes pleasure in finding a way to create gratuitous products. (25)

Where Bourdieu sees an acquired *habitus*, a set of defined behavioural skills shaped through the systems of family, school, class and work and Foucault sees a panoptic method of controlling the individual through organisation, classification and surveillance, Certeau understands that we all have the skills and capacity to transgress behavioural codes and evade surveillance in a small-scale guerrilla warfare against the imposed structures of order. The tactics of the dominated have no organised base of operations, but are formed 'on the wing', grasping at chances and chinks in the system; a rebel army striking against an all-encompassing empire. No matter that my friend's upbringing and education had encouraged a work ethic of success through diligence and that his supervisors stressed the penalties for those who failed to pull their weight as team players: in a small, everyday act of resistance, he realised that the panoptic eye had not, yet, reached the men's toilets.

Walking in the city

If the system of control is a city, then *bricolage*, 'the artisan-like inventiveness' of the dominated individual, can be seen as the '*lignes d'erre*', the wandering lines and indirect trajectories we trace through the grid of streets. 'The act of walking is to the urban system what the speech act is to language or to the statements uttered' – that is, it represents an imaginative expression within a set of conventions – and works as 'a process of appropriation on the part of the pedestrian (just as the speaker appropriates and takes on the language).' Certeau extends this metaphor in an often beautiful sequence which equates window-shopping and wandering with the speaker's 'turns of phrase' and 'stylistic figures'; in 'composing' our route we are creating and manipulating within the ordered map of the city, writing our own 'long poem of walking'. We read our own individual memories and associations into the 'official' names of streets and buildings, sometimes allowing these personal interpretations to shape our route; Certeau speaks of a friend from Sevres who, when in Paris, finds himself erring involuntarily towards the *rue de Sevres* and another who will not walk on streets which have names rather than numbers and whose path through the city is decided by this idiosyncratic pattern of preference. If Certeau's friends seem extreme cases, we can surely all think of our own unconscious detours away from the site of an unwelcome memory, or the images we fondly attach to, say, the Angel, London Fields and Limehouse in London, or elsewhere Route 66, Strawberry Fields and Zoo Station. Certeau brings his own examples from Paris:

> A strange toponymy that is detached from actual places and flies high over the city like a foggy geography of 'meanings' held in suspension, directing the physical deambulations below: *Place de L'Etoile, Concorde, Poissonniere* ... These constellations of names provide traffic patterns: they are stars directing intineraries ... a whole series of comparisons would be necessary to account for the magical powers proper names enjoy. (104)

Just as, when reading a novel, we visualise the fictional interiors, the layout of doors and the decoration in terms of rooms we know ourselves and thus perform a small act of creation with every page we read, so our 'long poem of walking' is also a constant process of invention and imagination. It seems fitting that the French Situationist movement saw the *derive*, or act of wandering through the city, as a legitimate work of art.

Problems with Certeau

Certeau's notions are evocative and romantic – perhaps to a fault. It is appealing to think that we were all practising inventive and creative resistant tactics without realising it, but where does this really leave us? Certeau is happy to celebrate the activity of those 'who have to get along in a network of already established forces', the manipulation of a dominant order 'without any illusion that it will change any time soon'. But this struggle to just 'get along' smacks of resignation. If we are satisfied with such small-scale activities as *la perruque*, if we call writing love-letters in company time 'subversion' and elevate walking in the city to an act of rebellion, we are unlikely to see any genuine transformation in the social order. Certeau is left championing the skill of using proverbs adeptly, or the child who 'scrawls and daubs on his schoolbooks ... he has made a space for himself'. In some lights, the 'art of making do' seems a sad testament to a mentality which accepts its own subordination and buckles down to make the best of it, scoring only the most minor, tokenistic victories against the systems of control.

This, of course, is a problem fundamental to the fragmented 'micropolitics' which succeeded post-marxism as the dominant paradigm of cultural studies and, as we shall see, it applies equally to the work of Janice Radway, Henry Jenkins and in particular to John Fiske.

Further reading

If Michel de Certeau's work has been less influential than that of Bourdieu and Foucault on cultural studies outside France, this is perhaps due to the comparative lack of translation. In addition to *The Practice of Everyday Life, The Writing of History* (first published 1974; University of Columbia Press, 1988) and *The Mystic Fable* (first published 1982; University of Chicago Press, 1992) are among the few currently available in English.

I have found Jeremy Ahearne's *Michel de Certeau: Interpretation And Its Other* (Polity Press, 1995) to be a useful and possibly unique study of Certeau's theory. This is, however, a sophisticated overview and might be offputting to those just beginning to engage with Certeau's work. Ian Buchanan, in *New Formations* 31, addresses criticisms of Certeau's theory and answers those who accuse *The Practice of Everyday Life* of presenting binary oppositions between oppressor and oppressed. As well as proposing a more fluid interpretation of the relation between 'strategy' and 'tactics', he also re-evaluates the importance of '*la perruque*' for its power to transform structure from within, rather than as a token act of minor resistance.

Certeau's scenario of walking as a tactic is taken up in Anne Friedberg's work on '*flanerie*', or the art of strolling, in *Window Shopping: Cinema and the Postmodern* (University of California Press, 1994). It also finds intriguing echoes in the fiction of Paul Auster, such as *City of Glass* (published by Faber in the *New York Trilogy*, 1987). Finally, the suggestion that we all engage in 'punk' *bricolage* could be extended further into the realm of cyberpunk. 'The street finds its own uses for things', says cyberpunk writer William Gibson, and his recent novels *Virtual Light* and *Idoru* in particular have much to say about the role of improvisation within both urban and information networks.

Links in this book

Aside from the clear links with Foucault and Bourdieu, the most obvious connection here is with Henry Jenkins' *Textual Poachers*, discussed in the next chapter. Jenkins pays explicit homage to Certeau, drawing extensively and productively on his theories of small-scale resistance to examine the relationship between science fiction fans and television producers. These strategies of negotiation also chime with Morley's approach to the television audience and Hebdige's subcultural improvisation and inform John Fiske and Janice Radway's theory of active 'readership' below; indeed, Fiske has named Certeau as an important influence on his own work.

6 | STATES OF RECEPTION

Negotiating the popular: John Fiske

As suggested in the last chapter, cultural studies reached the United States through a filter of French theory – Bourdieu, Foucault and de Certeau – whose stress on a decentred micropolitics of society had greater relevance to the complex and fragmented cultures of 1980s North America than the earlier, more localised and predominantly class-based British investigations. In practice, cultural studies in the USA has developed as a mutated anthropology: an investigation into the urban tribes of sunbathers, mall shoppers, 'Trekkies' and romance readers which interrogates popular cultures and 'subcultural' fangroups. As such, it brings the unseen – the trivial, the homemade, the 'minority' reading – to light, and frequently makes the familiar seem alien. This chapter represents a sample, chosen partly to demonstrate the focus on culturally disenfranchised social groups which typifies American cultural studies from this recent period and remains one of its strongest suits. Despite the shifts in content and emphasis, these studies nevertheless have in common with both their French and British counterparts a grounding in issues of cultural power and its relation to media representation, although here that concern inevitably extends to different cultural groups, such as midwestern housewives, West Coast youth and nationwide communities of gay science fiction fans.

John Fiske's work on the quintessential landscapes and landmarks of the 1980s were highly influential and established him as something of a heavyweight in the field, although others, including Henry Jenkins below, have questioned his optimism in the supposedly transformative power of audience readings.

Reading the Popular (1989)

Games and theories

While my references here are primarily to *Reading the Popular* alone, much of my comment in this chapter applies equally to its companion text, *Understanding Popular Culture*, which was published simultaneously and takes a similar format. Although Fiske stresses their differences in structure, both share a project of analysing geographically specific case studies from America and Australia through the lens of European theory. As such the two books provide a perfect example of the way cultural studies was exported from its home contexts – Fiske cites Stuart Hall, Michel de Certeau, Pierre Bourdieu and Roland Barthes as key influences – and mapped onto new cultural experiences. The case studies in both books, described by Fiske as 'a bricolage of frozen moments ... a series of snapshots taken by an academic on his intercontinental wanderings in the 1980s', have a fragmented, mix-and-match eclecticism about them but add up to a coherent document, a photograph album from the late 1980s and a clear theoretical argument about texts and audiences.

Fiske's view of 'popular culture' demonstrates the extent to which the associations of such key terms have changed in the thirty years since *The Uses of Literacy*. While Hoggart deplored the creeping Americanisation of popular life and its increasing saturation with crudely mass-produced artefacts, Fiske revels in the most blatantly commercial products – Levi's, tabloids, game shows, Madonna – and applauds their widespread consumption. The key to this seemingly dramatic change in attitude towards 'mass' texts is the change in attitude towards 'mass' audiences which emerged through Hall's Birmingham crew – Morley and Hebdige's view of negotiation and appropriation, for instance – and French theorists such as Certeau, with his models of readers 'making do' and scavenging their own meanings.

So Fiske is able to celebrate texts which earlier commentators would have detested because he sees meaning as generated not by the texts themselves, but by their reception; that is, they gain meaning only when used by audiences, through circulation and appropriation. We will see a similar idea below in Henry Jenkins' story about the 'Velveteen Rabbit', who learned that toys only become 'real' when they are loved and played with. To Fiske, 'texts, which are crucial in this process, need to be understood not by and for themselves but in their inter-relationships with other texts and with social life, for that is how their circulation is ensured.' If they are taken up by audiences and become part of everyday life – a soap opera whose plot twists are discussed at work every morning, or a comedy show whose catchphrases echo across school playgrounds – they will acquire popular meaning and survive; if they don't invite this kind of engagement, they will flop. Texts are 'inadequate in themselves ... they are completed only when taken up by people and inserted into their everyday culture.'

Popular culture then, comes from 'below', from the viewers, not from 'above'; popularity cannot be manufactured. We might answer that producers can surely make a fair attempt to capture various audience groups by deliberately, even cynically catering to recognised tastes and desires – for instance, the inclusion of a hit song on a film soundtrack, or the tokenistic introduction of a gay character to a television drama, or the recruiting of a 'boy band' according to an established formula – but Fiske chooses not to deal with issues of actual ownership or marketing.

This model of audiences resisting, opposing, negotiating and manipulating the culture handed down from the 'dominant' establishment is familiar from Birmingham – Fiske cites Stuart Hall on the relationship between the 'power-bloc and the people' – and from Certeau's notion of strategies and tactics, of workers' small, improvisatory strikes against the rigid framework of rules surrounding them; it also links back to Foucault's structures of power and corresponding forces of resistance. What Fiske does with it is bold and very possibly over-enthusiastic. He rates textual 'readings', or interpretations, as quasi-political acts, stressing their power to challenge representation and structures of meaning. Interpretations 'against the grain', that is, contrary to the meaning intended by the producers, lead viewers to a sense of empowerment which may lead them to make minor but crucial changes in their everyday lives. Fiske gives the example of female *Cagney and Lacey* fans whose reading of the series gave them increased confidence and proposes that teenage girls who find pleasure in Madonna's power over her own image may make 'political progress ... in their relationships with their boyfriends.'

This may sound reasonable enough, but Fiske goes on to recommend this type of 'semiotic resistance' over conventional methods of protest. He describes the process of 'thinking differently' enabled by resistant readings as an 'erosive force' on the 'macro' level of society, 'weakening the system from within so that it is more amenable to change at the structural level'. Rather than direct opposition, such as members of the CCCS might well have supported, Fiske advocates 'improving the lot of the subordinate rather than changing the system that subordinates them'. Everything that was problematic in Certeau's model of 'making do' is amplified by Fiske's implication that talking back to a television programme may be ultimately more politically effective than taking to the streets. We might be able to accept terms like 'semiotic resistance' and the association of struggles over meaning with metaphorical 'skirmishes' and 'terrain', but to claim such activities as genuine political struggle will be hard for some to swallow.

To be fair, Fiske does accept the limits of this 'micro-politics', with its stress on gradual rather than radical change; but his unqualified association of audience readings with 'resistance' and this resistance with the socially 'progressive', haunts all his work from this period, finds echoes in the work of his contemporaries, like Radway, and has become a stumbling-block for later theorists such as Jenkins.

Case study: video games

Fiske does have one thing in common with Hoggart's work of thirty years previously; both now have an air of poignant nostalgia. This is more of a paradox in Fiske than in *The Uses of Literacy*, which was, in part, meant as a souvenir of times past and it is perhaps a sign of the increasingly rapid turnover of contemporary culture that Fiske's references to President Reagan and Pac-Man, topical at the time of writing, now seem to recall a distant era.

The connection between these two 1980s icons is that Reagan was apparently one of the few public figures to praise video games and the arcades in which they appeared. The dominant, 'establishment' view of the time was that arcades, or 'parlours' as they were known in Australia, led young people to waste time and money, encouraged delinquency and fostered addiction. A framework of prohibition was therefore established around both the activity and the environment and, of course, a corresponding resistance emerged as a direct result; which is to say that teenage boys were drawn to arcades precisely because of the image of rebellion they had acquired. Fiske identifies the possibilities offered by arcades for 'evading the social control exercised by the home-school-work nexus' and the opportunities they embody for 'the subordinate, the young user of the arcade ... of adopting an alternative cultural stance'.

So far, this case study is an exemplary mapping of previous theory – Paul Willis and Dick Hebdige's investigations into disillusioned British youth, Foucault and Certeau's paradigms of power and resistance – onto a fresh new cultural area. Fiske draws on contemporary newspaper reports, a 1982 guide to better gameplay and apparently, some ethnographic research in order to build up a portrait of a disenfranchised, subordinate, often non-white male who finds, in the machines, a means of expression, identity and self-worth. The 'machinist', to use Fiske's dynamic term, enters a different sphere when he grasps the joystick and touches the fire button; he passes into a world where he can control meanings, where he can hone his skills towards personal triumph and reputation. The video game guidebook recognises this by promising the reader that he will become the 'Arcade Aristocrat', and Perth's largest chain of arcades is also canny in naming itself 'Timezone': this is a different space, away from home and work where the machine is a television or an assembly-line.

Yet that name also suggests a problem. The arcade is a remote space, with no relation to the outside world, and the skills it encourages are virtually meaningless outside its doors. When Jim from Nashville says of his Pac-Man tactics, 'big bonus for small action – that's what life's all about, isn't it?', Fiske comments that Jim's life probably involves very few big bonuses, but concludes that, although the reward here is only illusory and has no bearing on Jim's real societal position, the game 'may well leave a residue of subversion that remains in the subject, to the discomfort of the social controllers.' We are back to micropolitics, erosion and wishful thinking.

Fiske also notes the irony that the arcade actually enforces control, with its rules about eating, drinking and dress codes, but again, this doesn't change his enthusiasm for the 'resistance' he identifies. There is little made of the fact that the arcade itself is owned and run by the capitalist 'establishment', no matter that experienced players can extend the amount of game-time they get for a single coin, or that the game's scenarios are invariably in accordance with 'dominant' culture. 'Nowhere do we find video representations of Ronald Reagan and Margaret Thatcher to be blasted out of the skies', he admits, going on to note that there are, on the contrary, games involving 'the rape of women, or the Ku Klux Klan catching and lynching "niggers"'. These last shocking observations are allowed to just slip by, without a thought for the 'pleasures' and 'empowerment' they might offer young working-class men, or precisely the type of 'identity' they might be forming.

Case study: Madonna

Of course, you could hardly claim to be involved with cultural studies at all in the late 1980s unless you had a chapter on Madonna and in this Fiske does not disappoint. The actual content may have less effect now than it did, due to the repetition of the same ideas, watered-down, in Sunday supplements, fan magazines and undergraduate essays, but again this chapter is a good example of Fiske's arguments and their flaws.

Madonna is seen as disrupting 'dominant' frameworks of masculinity and femininity, as denying patriarchy's conventions for representing women – even when appearing in *Playboy* – and as offering her teenage female fans a source of empowerment. 'Madonna offers some young girls the opportunity to find meanings of their own feminine sexuality that suit them, meanings that are "independent"'; meanings which resist the patriarchal labels of 'slut' and 'tart'. So Lucy, 'a 14-year-old fan', comments that 'she's tarty and seductive … but it looks alright when she does it, you know'. Cynics might note that Fiske had a fourteen-year-old daughter called Lucy at the time of writing.

The crucial question here is whether all audience readings are automatically 'resistant' and in turn whether we should be so quick to judge them as 'progressive'. It's true that Fiske finds some valid examples where Madonna's image is used by teenage girls in scenarios of lighthearted rebellion and confidence. What he fails to consider is the very real possibility for alternative readings, for instance those suggested by the *Playboy* feature with its caption about the artiste's 'sopping sex'. If girls can gain self-esteem through Madonna's image, isn't it possible that teenage boys may gain their own empowerment and pleasure through the conventional, patriarchal meanings which Madonna's ambiguous persona also contains? If those boys take their readings – which despite their basis in a subordinate group, are not necessarily 'resistant' or 'progressive' – into everyday life, might their improvised culture not include treating Madonna wannabes as sluts and tarts? Might these readings of Madonna as confident, available tease not have a very real 'social' effect in terms of its influence on the power relations between young men and women on the street, or by extension a 'political' effect in its bearing on, say, legal judgments on cases of sexual assault? My argument is not that Fiske's identification of positive, encouraging readings is misguided or invalid, but that in his haste to champion all audience interpretation he too frequently ignores the more problematic implications of this localised creativity.

Problems with Fiske

I have taken John Fiske so much to task that it would be churlish to repeat the charges again. Suffice it to say that his example of 'the kids who sang jeeringly at a female student of mine as she walked past them in a short skirt and heels', who are applauded for their 'cheeky resistive subcultural purposes', has become notorious and illustrates, better than any other passage, Fiske's selective blindness of this period.

Further reading

Understanding Popular Culture and *Reading the Popular* were both published by Routledge in 1989 and have been reprinted many times since. *Television Culture*, originally published by Methuen in 1987, works along similar lines, but as the title suggests, with a narrower subject matter; *Reading Television* (Methuen, 1978) is of interest because it represents a collaborative authorship with the young John Hartley, whose work is discussed in more detail below.

Two major theorists used by Fiske but absent from this book are Michel Bakhtin and Umberto Eco; the first is best known for his theories of carnival, which relate to Fiske's piece on wrestling and the latter has written widely on popular texts and the process of reading. Bakhtin's *Rabelais and His World* (1968) and Eco's *The Role of the Reader* (1981) would be good starting-points for further investigation.

Links in this book

Obviously, Fiske draws on Hall, Certeau and Foucault for his theoretical framework. He also references Paul Willis on disaffected youth cultures and Angela McRobbie on the trials and insecurities of female adolescence; Bourdieu is mentioned along the way and Barthes is relevant to his discussion, in *Understanding Popular Culture*, of 'Rock'n'Wrestling'. As mentioned above, Henry Jenkins sounds a note of caution against Fiske's optimism in *Textual Poachers*.

Feminism and the romance: Janice Radway

Reading the Romance (1984)

Reading the Romance struggles desperately to resolve its own contradictions, and never succeeds; yet it is all the more honest and enduringly complex because of this apparent failure. Radway states early on that her project is to 'argue that romance reading is a profoundly conflicted activity centered upon a profoundly conflicted form'. The irony is, of course, that this profound conflict attains another level as Radway herself, a middle-class feminist and academic, veers between deploring the reactionary aspects of popular romance fiction on working-class women and applauding the small victories it helps them attain; between validating the power of the reader to make her own meanings and advocating, on the other hand, that these readers should be 'guided' towards feminism by their more educated sisters.

Even the book's method involves a combination of approaches which again complicate but also expand its range of findings: unlike Fiske, Radway considers the 'institutional matrix' of the romance, from the technology of printing and glue through ownership and marketing, and attempts a purely textual breakdown of the 'ideal' romance formula which moves through structural analysis to lists and even diagrams. As in much feminist cultural theory of this period – see also McRobbie – there is also an attempt to shoehorn psychoanalysis into the discussion, in the form of a notion about romance-reading enacting 'the ongoing search for the mother', which with hindsight seems superfluous and distracting.

What distinguishes *Reading the Romance*, though, is its central section of ethnographic research based on a network of working-class women in the midwestern town of Smithton. Radway's guide and initial contact was Dot Evans, a forty-eight-year-old woman in a lavender pants suit whose work at a local bookstore, recommending and reviewing romantic paperbacks, had made her a focal point for the female readers of the community. Radway's research involved taped interviews with Dot and her clients, a series of questionnaires, a fieldwork journal and long-term observation. This diligent undercover work results in an immensely detailed and vivid account of Smithton's women, peppered with statistics, descriptions of lifestyle and lengthy transcripts of dialogue which read almost like soap opera.

Dot: He starts stalking her and this is visually …
Kit: It's hysterical.
Dot: You can see it.
Kit: She's backin' off.
Dot: She's trying to get to the stairway to get to her room.
Kit: And make a mad dash.
Ann: She's what they call a 'petite pocket Venus type'. (80)

While Radway is obviously accepted into the community, she retains through her role as researcher a certain academic distance and by extension a sense of 'difference' – otherwise, why would Dot have to stress to others that 'Jan is just people!' This feeling of the author's dual persona, on the one hand bonding with women as a 'reader' and on the other backing off to study them as a 'writer', contributes subtly to the book's sense of troubled conscience.

Pro

Radway's main point in support of romance-reading, and one that she keeps repeating almost as if to reassure herself, is that the very act of finding a space and time for a 'selfish' pleasure operates for these women as a 'declaration of independence'. Most of the women Radway questioned cited 'escape' as one of the main pleasures of reading, no matter what the actual content – Dot goes so far as to confess that 'I think my body is in the room but the rest of me is not (when I am reading)' – an observation which, like so many in *Reading the Romance*, turns out to be double-edged.

While this claiming of space in a domestic life primarily devoted to the needs of others clearly has a social importance, Radway's further arguments for the value of romance-reading are not always entirely convincing. Because authors are presumed to research their books thoroughly, Radway claims they serve an 'educational' purpose for the Smithton women – one is quoted as having learned from a romance set in an 'eye hospital' the differences between English and American medical systems, while another agrees that romances can provide recipes for 'fancy dishes … you really learn something'. The blind faith of these readers in the authority of romance authors – 'I never *thought* of questioning it!', 'I just assumed they research like the devil' – and the substitution of trivia for education and travel seems an ultimately rather sad, limiting exchange, even if it does enable the women to impress their husbands with snippets of information.

Some of the women in Smithton have plans to write their own novels – one is undertaking her own research into 'Indian Ways' – which on paper looks like an excellent example of the transformative power of romance-reading and its potential to forge self-esteem; but we might ask how many published authors have actually emerged from Smithton, and whether this enthusiasm on a small scale can have any effect on the larger systems of ownership and power, which Radway has earlier described as involving 'young women with master's degrees in literature' deciding what will be read by midwestern housewives.

We are back to the arena of 'micropolitics', and whether Radway's findings in Smithton seem encouraging or vaguely depressing will depend on the extent to which we see minor personal triumphs as vital ingredients in a bigger picture of social change. It is hard to argue against the case studies she presents where Smithton women have been prompted by their reading to increase their own self-esteem and 'develop assertive techniques in a few restricted areas of their lives'. Dot and her friends relate the story of June Anderson, whose husband believed 'that the gods were talking to him ... she was under his thumb'.

> Dot: She was makin' his life one slide, buttered well! And here he
> was, you know, thinkin', 'boy my house is in tip-top shape.'
> Ann: Yup.
> Dot: And then she got ahold of books and it's been really a shame!
> (102)

The key phrase, though, is 'a few restricted areas' and Radway knows this as well as anyone.

Contra

As a feminist and academic, Radway 'knows' that the traditional romance encourages and validates patriarchal myths: that a woman can only find happiness in marriage, through submission to a dominant man and finally by succumbing to the male ideal of wife and domestic, however spunky she may be up until the last chapter. 'It is tempting to suggest that romantic fiction must be an active agent in the maintenance of the status quo because it ultimately reconciles women to patriarchal society and reintegrates them with its institutions.' This would be the conventional feminist, or for that matter, academic view of romance fiction and it is to her credit that Radway's study successfully and enduringly disrupts this stereotype. It's no less to her credit that she is unable to provide an alternative theory, although it does prevent any neat solutions. Though she is convinced of romance-reading's potential to build confidence and enable small resistances within the home, and the novels' openness to 'oppositional' readings which stress the heroine's independence and achievement rather than her eventual taming, Radway nevertheless has to ask whether romances defuse women's dissatisfaction, 'deflecting and recontaining real protest'. As such they would provide an illusory, temporary solution to a real need; indeed, on several occasions she compares romance novels to 'tranquilisers'.

> In the end, the romance-reading process gives the reader a strategy for making her present situation more comfortable without substantive reordering of its structure rather than a comprehensive program for reorganising her life in such a way that all needs might be met. (215)

This is the crux of the issue with regard to what Radway later calls 'the limited but ... creative ways in which people resist the deleterious effects of their social situations'; we have come across it before in Certeau's 'making do', as well as in Fiske. These small-scale readings and resistances make life more bearable as it is, while avoiding any fundamental change in the system. Whether Radway's conclusion offers a way out of this impasse is open to debate.

The Romance and feminism

> Because I suspect a demand for real change in power relations will occur only if women also come to understand that their need for romances is a function of their dependent status *as women* and of their acceptance of marriage as the only route to female fulfillment, I think we as feminists might help this change along by first learning to recognize that romance reading originates in very real dissatisfaction and embodies a valid, if limited, protest. Then, by developing strategies for making that dissatisfaction and its causes consciously available to romance readers and by learning how to encourage that process in such a way that it will be delivered in the arena of actual social relations rather than acted out in the imagination, we might join hands with women who are, after all, our sisters. (220)

This passage comes very near to the end of *Reading the Romance*, and I have quoted it in full because of its importance to the questions raised above. The result of Radway's research, we see, is ultimately to conclude that the small-scale resistance she observes in Smithton is simply not enough; it is 'limited', 'acted out in the imagination' rather than in the social arena. Although she welcomes the minor changes in the women's lives which seem to have been prompted by romance-reading, Radway goes further than Fiske and asks for 'real change in power relations'. The problem lies in where she sees this change originating. After being accepted as 'just people' by Dot and her comrades, Radway has come home to the academy and now speaks to an audience very different from the Smithton women; the 'we' of this passage refers not to romance-readers but to female academics, the type who would buy *Reading the Romance* rather than *The Flame and the Flower* or *Blades of Passion*. Her need to remind the reader that the Smithton women are 'after all, our sisters' enforces, rather than erodes, the barriers of class, education and geography between this 'us' and 'them', while the proposal to encourage and guide romance readers into a more effective protest by showing them their own dissatisfaction is clearly well-meant but might well be received as patronising. It is ironic that following such an involved, ground-level and long-term piece of undercover research into the rituals and customs of her chosen community, the final impression is one of distance between the romance-readers and the writer.

Problems with Radway

Henry Jenkins, while praising Radway's study as 'exemplary', notes the paradox discussed immediately above; Radway casts writers 'as vanguard intellectuals who might lead the fans toward a more overtly political relationship to popular culture. Academic distance has thus allowed scholars either to judge or to instruct but not to converse with the fan community, a process which requires greater proximity and the surrender of certain intellectual pretensions and institutional privileges.' Yet as I argue below, Jenkins' own approach could be seen as sacrificing a critical objectivity for the sake of greater trust and acceptance among fans. Where Radway is able to retreat out of Smithton, most of Jenkins' adult life, including his own romances, has been tied up in television fandom; his admission that he feels 'a high degree of responsibility and accountability' to the groups he discusses, and looks at his fellow fans 'as active collaborators in the research process' could be regarded as a problematic move to the other end of the scale. This dilemma still faces contemporary researchers into popular culture – not just those involved in ethnography, but those increasing numbers of academics who are attempting to theorise about popular texts they have loved since childhood. There is an inevitable schizophrenia about such projects which neither Radway nor Jenkins fully resolve. Nevertheless, Radway shows here that the most stimulating work can emerge from contradiction and the admission of problems, rather than from easy solutions.

Further reading

Janice Radway is joint editor of *The Oxford Companion to Women's Writing In The United States* (Oxford University Press, 1995) and more recently published *A Feeling For Books*, on the Book-of-the-Month Club (University of North Carolina, 1997). She currently edits the Routledge journal *Cultural Studies* with Lawrence Grossberg.

Finally, Radway uses two sources which fall outside the scope of this book, but which nevertheless deserve mention as classic texts within their fields: Stanley Fish's *Is There A Text In This Class?* (Harvard, 1980), on reader interpretation and Clifford Geertz's *The Interpretation of Cultures* (Basic Books, 1973), on anthropological investigation, provide worthwhile avenues for further study.

Links in this book

Fiske and Jenkins are immediately relevant to *Reading the Romance*, as my frequent cross-referencing during this chapter must have shown. The work Radway herself refers to most, though, is that of David Morley and Angela McRobbie on *Nationwide* and teenage girls respectively. She also draws on the research of Paul Willis, Charlotte Brunsdon and Dorothy Hobson, who are also mentioned above in the CCCS section; further proof of Birmingham's mighty influence on American cultural studies.

Powers of fandom: Henry Jenkins

Textual Poachers (1992)

The trouble with 'Trekkies'

Henry Jenkins bravely opens this attempt to demonstrate the sophistication of television fans by describing a group of 'Trekkies' – the inverted commas are important, as we'll see – meeting their hero, William Shatner. The fans are 'nerdy guys with glasses and rubber Vulcan ears,

"I Grok Spock" T-shirts stretched over their bulging stomachs. One man laughs maliciously about a young fan he has just met who doesn't know Yeoman Rand's cabin number, while his friend mumbles about the great buy he got on a DeForest Kelly album.' Of course, as the accompanying photograph makes clear, this is a parody from the American show *Saturday Night Live* rather than a real convention and Jenkins uses it as his springboard to analyse the conventional image of the television fan. Fans, Jenkins concludes from the television sketch and an equally scathing article in *Newsweek* magazine, 'are characterized as "kooks", obsessed with trivia, celebrities and collectibles; as misfits and "crazies"; as "a lot of overweight women, a lot of divorced and single women"'. Indeed, a skim through *Textual Poachers* might do little to alter the prejudices of the cynical reader. The book is liberally illustrated with fan-portraits of Bodie and Doyle from the British *Professionals* series and the covers of fanzines devoted to assistants from the BBC's *Doctor Who*, while a *Star Trek* 'filk song' exults 'I was with the Midwest crowd/Who stood in line for blocks ... and we talked for three days running/Of how Khan did push his luck/And I am saved!' That the authors of these fan texts are predominantly female may lend further support to the *Newsweek* stereotype.

Jenkins' response, at its simplest, is to reject the stereotype of 'Trekkies' for their preferred term, 'Trekkers'. Through this crucial shift in terminology he seeks to replace the image of cultural dupes and misfits with a portrait of an active, creative community who perform complex negotiations both on the level of textual meaning – for instance, interpreting the relationship between Kirk and Spock as homoerotic – and on a socio-political level – lobbying NBC for the series' return in the late 1960s, or campaigning for the representation of gay characters in *The Next Generation*. While *Star Trek* remains one of the key texts in fandom and 'Trekkers' may represent the most established and longstanding fan community, the skills and powers which Jenkins attributes to them are, he claims, shared by devotees of *The Prisoner*, *The Man From UNCLE*, *The Equaliser* and *Miami Vice*. The fact that many readers who accept the cultural validity of the first examples may blanch at the latter suggestions demonstrates the prejudices and hierarchies of 'taste' which persist even at this late stage within cultural studies.

Theories

Before engaging with fan texts themselves, Jenkins provides an exemplary survey of the existing key studies on audiences and their relations to popular culture, noting their relevance to his own project and assessing their pros and cons. He picks Radway up, for instance, for her sometimes 'distanced' perspective on romance readers, which leads her to regard them as passive and in need of guidance towards a more politicised response. David Morley's *Nationwide* study also comes under mild criticism for its assumption that audience interpretations which differ from the producers' intended meaning are 'misreadings', and furthermore that only Morley himself, as an academic, can decide what the 'official', scholarly interpretation should be. Morley, of course, was influenced by Hall's model of dominant, negotiated and oppositional readings, which Jenkins critiques in turn. To assume that an audience reading which contradicts that of the producers is necessarily 'oppositional' is a simplification. Jenkins argues that the relationship is far more complex and fluid, showing through his example of the television series *Beauty and the Beast* that while fans clearly feel an initial close affinity towards their chosen programme, they may move in and out of harmony with the producers in a pattern of alternate frustration and enthusiasm, sometimes applauding the 'official' direction and sometimes preferring their own home-made plotlines, but always working within the programme's original framework. Jenkins boldly asserts that 'readers are not *always* resistant' and further that '*all* resistant readings are not necessarily progressive readings'; an iminently sensible reminder which many commentators, perhaps most notably John Fiske in the works I discussed earlier, seem to forget in their enthusiasm to find a subversive 'micropolitics' in any and all audience interpretation.

Jenkins' theorist of choice, then, is none of the above, but rather Michel de Certeau, who provides him with the central metaphor that fans are 'like the poachers of old': operating on the margins but skilled at appropriating and making do from what they salvage, comparatively powerless as individuals but collectively able to make the establishment take notice. Jenkins reminds us about Certeau's theory of reading as 'advances and retreats, tactics and games played with the text':

> ... a type of cultural bricolage through which readers fragment texts
> and reassemble the broken shards according to their own blueprints,
> salvaging bits and pieces of the found material in making sense of
> their own social experience. (26)

In a way, of course, this is what Jenkins, like any other contemporary cultural theorist, is doing himself with the body of existing theory; sifting through, assessing the value of various points, taking up or discarding when it seems appropriate to his own project. Touchingly, though, Jenkins draws his final support not from a theoretical text but from the children's story 'The Velveteen Rabbit', by Margery Williams Bianco. Rather than corrupting popular texts through their endless re-viewing, sampling, improvisation and reworking, Jenkins proposes that fans are doing to their favourite programmes what children do to their most precious toys; making them 'real' through play and love. Adorno, Jenkins explains, would see this process as vandalism and slow destruction; Jenkins views it as 'traces of fondly remembered experiences, evidence of ... having held the toy too long or pet it too often, in short, marks of its loving use.' Given such a choice between cultural positions, it's hard not to take his side.

Powers

We have seen that Jenkins distances himself from the kind of Fiskean idealism which is too quick to applaud any divergent audience reading as 'resistant' and potentially 'progressive'. However, in many respects Jenkins entertains a more positive view than Fiske about audience capabilities. Fiske celebrates the 'power' of viewers to challenge intended readings and produce their own interpretations, and praises the act of appropriation as a small-scale victory in the constant skirmish over cultural meanings. Compared to the power of the producers to enforce their own interpretation, not just through the 'official' text but through intertextual material such as posters, toys, interviews and house magazines, these textual victories seem minor indeed. To give an obvious example, the Fiske of *Understanding Popular Culture* might glory in the 'resistance' shown by a household of gay men who cheer whenever Kirk lays his hand on Spock's shoulder; but this small-scale pleasure, confined to a living-room, does nothing to prevent the producers of the *Star Trek* film series from matching both characters up with female love interest or encouraging Shatner to stress in interviews that Kirk is not and has never been gay.

By contrast, Jenkins insists that fans do have powers beyond the textual level, and that their struggle over meanings can extend to a social arena. Fans develop networks of communication and distribution through which to circulate their readings, or campaign in order to have their interpretations recognised in the 'official' text, rather than remaining confined to the microsphere of personal interpretation. In part, this wider dissemination and recognition of audience readings is achieved through fanzines and conventions, or more recently internet bulletin boards and newsgroups, as we shall see below. At crucial moments, though, fan culture goes so far as to enter into direct contact and conflict with the producers of a show or the network executives responsible for cancellation, arguing with all the conviction of any minority protest group that their views be respected.

> Many have traced the emergence of an organized media fan culture to late 1960s efforts to pressure NBC into returning *Star Trek* to the air, a movement which has provided a model for more recent attempts to reverse network decisions, such as the highly publicized efforts to save *Beauty and the Beast* or *Cagney and Lacey* … American *Doctor Who* supporters volunteer their time at PBS stations across the country, trying to translate their passion for the program into pledge drive contributions that will ensure its continued airing … COOP, a national *Twin Peaks* organization, employed local rallies and computer networking to try to keep that doomed series on the air. (28)

If these campaigns seem trivial, or more importantly seem to trivialise the efforts of 'genuine' political groups by using the tools and language of protest merely to sustain a television programme, we should remember that the focus of the 'Gaylaxian' group, as Jenkins discusses in his later *Science Fiction Audiences*, was to insist on the representation of gay characters in *The Next Generation* and that, in some ways, they appeared to succeed. If the two 'gay' episodes offered by the writers treated homosexuality through extended metaphor, rather than direct portrayal, that is perhaps the nature of the skirmish between producers and fans; we can hardly expect landowners to hand rabbits over to the poachers without a fight.

Documents

This kind of direct engagement is just one aspect of fan culture as Jenkins describes it. Another level of the fan community, less confrontational but no less active, is concerned not with lobbying for change to the 'official' text but with creating a wealth of 'unofficial' material whose number often far exceeds that of professionally-produced episodes, novelisations and magazines and whose subject matter frequently threatens or overflows the proscribed boundaries of the 'official' version. In stressing the importance of lasting documents and permanent records of interpretation to the fan community, Jenkins is actually arguing against Certeau, who regarded the reader's 'poached culture' as inherently temporary and transitory.

Certeau's view does not apply to fandom, Jenkins replies, partly because of the sense of community, in which meanings circulate, are shaped through discussion and remain in debate – as opposed to the solitary, isolated reader of Certeau's picture – and partly because fandom erodes the boundaries between reading and writing. Fans do not merely talk back to the screen, like those in many of Fiske's examples; they videotape the episode and then write a sequel, or freezeframe an image and work it into a modified portrait, or even find an editing suite and create a montage from several episodes, combined with an apposite soundtrack, which entirely alters the television show's 'intended' message. If nothing else, *Textual Poachers* is an invaluable testament to the rich variety of this fan culture and a laudable attempt to both preserve and circulate examples of fan-produced texts which, as Jenkins suggests, have existed for years as dog-eared, faintly lithographed pages of script or worn-out nth-generation copies of video art; the book includes leaflets, cartoons, video stills, extracts from unpublished novels and lovingly crafted drawings of television characters, all convincing evidence that 'active' interpretation can progress far beyond a fleeting moment of textual control to become a process of shared creativity which produces lasting artefacts. While this form of fan activity may not attempt to change the output of the network 'producers', it could be argued that such direct conflict has been made unnecessary by the fact that these fans are 'producers' themselves.

Slash

Of the fan texts Jenkins describes, the most intriguing subcategory must be 'slash', a genre of erotic fan fiction which centres on same-sex encounters between the protagonist of a popular series. That the title 'slash' derives from the oblique stroke in 'K/S', or 'Kirk/Spock', demonstrates once again a primary source in *Star Trek*; yet, while a tale of Spock and Kirk during the Vulcan mating fever opens Jenkins' account, he also provides vivid examples of slash between *Blake's 7*'s Vila and Avon, *The Man From UNCLE*'s Illya and Napoleon, even *The Professionals* – 'The crazy, tender melting Bodie could inspire in him when he was least expecting it no longer disconcerted Doyle ... Ray Doyle, well-known lover of ladies and all-round stud had fallen in love with his partner.'

That these extracts have the power to jolt and disturb a fan accustomed to the 'official' heterosexual coding of these programmes demonstrates the genuinely subversive nature of slash fiction. Jenkins explains that the authors of these stories, frequently professional married women, keep their identities secret for fear of losing their jobs and jeopardising their position; other fans have fiercely denounced this kind of fiction as 'character rape', while some producers, such as Lucasfilm with the *Star Wars* characters, insist that 'X-rated' stories about the cast are strictly prohibited by copyright. In many ways, then, slash can be regarded, unlike some other fan interpretation, as 'resistant' – as a body of readings circulated through an underground network, directly contravening both the official line of the producers and the consensus of 'official' fan meaning. Many conventions, Jenkins reports, refuse to allow homoerotic texts to be distributed for fear of upsetting actor guests and fellow fans.

Jenkins subsequently proposes that slash may be regarded not just as 'resistant' but as 'progressive' – a term which, remember, he does not bandy about lightly. Slash fiction stresses the sensuality of masculine bodies, with an emphasis on gentle cuddling and caressing rather than the tropes of penetration and ejaculation favoured by more conventional porn. In its portrayal of male sexual roles as fluid and changeable it breaks away from rigid codings of effeminate/butch, soft/hard or dominant/passive. Finally, Jenkins argues, it has a social, even politically significant aspect. Through the community of slash writers, middle-class straight women come into contact and dialogue with the often unfamiliar cultures of lesbians and bisexuals and many find themselves aligning with the principles of the gay movement. 'Not all of slash is progressive,' Jenkins admits; but in this case, it seems, the term could be used with some justification.

Problems with Jenkins

Jenkins, we have seen, criticises Morley's and Radway's studies of audience as overly reliant on an elitist 'scholarly' opinion, and stresses by contrast his own personal enthusiasm for fan texts and active involvement in the communities he discusses. It could be argued that this personal engagement takes his study to another, equally unhealthy extreme, whereby Jenkins is too ready to applaud even the most cackhanded and trivial artefacts of fan culture; hence the clumsy 'etc.' in a flyer for 'Anglofans' is read not as laziness but as foregrounding 'the group's constant and "unlimited" ability to accommodate new texts.' Jenkins' claim to have circulated chapters of *Textual Poachers* among the fans it describes, asking for their comments and altering the text accordingly, could also be seen as a bridge too far; surely some degree of critical distance is necessary and an author in Jenkins' position should not have to be afraid of upsetting the objects of his study. Finally, as Jenkins freely admits that his choice of graduate school programme, his 'budding romantic life' and of course his current academic career depend on his involvement in fandom, a cynical reader could be forgiven for greeting his more enthusiastic claims with 'well, he would say that, wouldn't he?' *Textual Poachers* never quite solves this dilemma, but of itself asks vital questions about the ideal position of the researcher to his or her subject, and the drawbacks as well as the advantages of being both fan and theorist at once.

For the sake of balance you might also want to consider Toby Miller's implicit critique of Jenkins' approach in *The Avengers* (BFI, 1997). Miller comments snippily on those members of the 'professoriate' whose 'attempts ... to rehabilitate fans include numbering themselves among the group ... licensing their own pleasures as professional acts of theory and critique, and claiming that the process is intensely risky, even academically death-defying. A vast array of conference papers, books and speaking fees suggests otherwise.' In fact the methods of Toby Miller, whose audience research in *The Avengers* consists largely of e-mailing his friends in the professoriate and quoting them without source or context, are equally open to criticism.

The debate around academic fandom and the relative merits of 'objective' distance and 'personal' involvement has not yet been resolved, but the issues are helpfully summarised in Jenkins' own introduction to *Hop On Pop* (Duke University Press, forthcoming 1999).

Further reading

With regard to this chapter, Henry Jenkins' most important work is *Science Fiction Audiences*, co-authored with John Tulloch (Routledge, 1995), which offers parallel studies of *Doctor Who* and *Star Trek* fandom through interviews and surveys, and develops the issues of queer reading raised by 'slash' through an investigation into the 'Gaylaxian' organisation.

Queer reading, as embodied in *Textual Poachers* by gay slash fiction, has become an area of great interest to cultural studies as a practice through which gay and lesbian audiences can lift their own homoerotic meanings and pleasures from an 'official', heterosexual text. While Jenkins tends to document the interpretations of others, many gay theorists have performed their own queer appropriations on popular texts and argued for the validity of this counter-interpretation. Andy Medhurst's essay on 'Batman, Deviance and Camp' is a particularly accessible example and can be found alongside an article by Jenkins in the excellent *The Many Lives of the Batman*, edited by Roberta Pearson and William Uricchio (Routledge, 1991). Other recent texts in the same vein include Paul Burston and Colin Richardson's *A Queer Romance: Lesbians, Gay Men and Popular Culture* (Routledge, 1995) and Alex Doty's *Making Things Perfectly Queer* (University of Minnesota Press, 1993), both of which overturn familiar popular texts with cheek and intelligence.

An intriguing supplement to *Textual Poachers* can be found in the final pages of *Enterprise Zones* (Westview Press, 1996) where one of the editors, Taylor Harrison, interviews Jenkins about fan reactions to the book, the ethics of 'poaching' from audience material and Jenkins' own relationship to the gay community.

Links in this book

Jenkins has been thorough in his examination of the field as it stood in the first years of the 1990s, and we have seen that *Textual Poachers* comments quite thorougly and critically on the earlier work of Hall, Certeau, Morley, Fiske and Radway. It only remains to note that his discussion of 'bad taste' as a socially rooted category, applied here to the 'Trekkies' of the opening chapter, makes appropriate use of Bourdieu to demonstrate that these concepts are far from natural, and that one of fandom's more disruptive powers is to muddle and blur the established lines between 'trash' and 'art.'

7 DOING CULTURAL STUDIES

Hartleyism

'Hartleyism', unlike, say, 'Arnoldian' or 'Leavisite', is a word I have just invented; but I feel it deserves coinage. John Hartley has, after all, been compared to 'Raymond Williams on roller-blades' and deemed 'the Kurt Vonnegut of Cultural Studies … the nearest thing there is to an acid trip', while Henry Jenkins, in turn, describes him as 'one part Dr Seuss, one part Hunter S. Thompson'. Hartley's prose, at least in his most recent works *The Politics of Pictures* and *Popular Reality*, is riddled with puns to make a tabloid editor wince – 'frocks pop', 'telebrity', 'tongue in chic' – and regularly makes connections between such diverse historical texts as a 1776 thesis by Tom Paine and a modern breakfast cereal on the basis that both are called 'Common Sense'. While this whimsy may irritate some readers, it also constitutes a discourse of cultural studies as distinctive and individual in its way as Hoggart's chatty, no-nonsense rhetoric or Williams' commanding arguments. Certainly, few other academic writers would begin a study of media publics with the words 'For many years, my father was a hairbrush. He, that is the hairbrush, was improbably made of perspex.'

Hartley is useful to my account because of his intersection, at several points, with the cultural studies 'heritage' I have been constructing, and his embracing, in turn, of new directions in the discipline. His enthusiasm to serve as a junction point between the past and future of cultural studies is suggested by his current position at the University of Cardiff, Wales, as head of the Tom Hopkinson Centre for Media Research – whose title celebrates the editor of *Picture Post* magazine – and as editor of the newly-created *International Journal of Cultural Studies*. Hartley's latest project is characteristic: *Uses of Television*, scheduled to be published forty years after the Hoggart text to which it pays homage.

John Hartley studied Hoggart and Hall in the late 1960s, then published with John Fiske in the late 1970s. He subsequently relocated to Australia and worked his way through the academic ranks at Murdoch University, transferring to Edith Cowan University and finally returning to the United Kingdom. Though he is now based in Cardiff, Hartley's two most recent books are built predominantly around Australian texts of the 1990s – Australian *Playboy*, the *West Australian* newspaper and Kylie Minogue – and he continues to associate with the people he calls the old quirks and young turks of Australian academia – among them Graeme Turner, McKenzie Wark, Tom O'Regan, Catharine Lumby, Tara Brabazon, Alan McKee and Mark Gibson – who are shaping into a formidable contingent within the international cultural studies of the late 1990s.

Not-Quiteness: an interview with John Hartley, February 1998

Cultural Studies: past and present

WB: *How would you trace the history and development of cultural studies to date, and how do you see your own place in that history?*

JH: Cultural studies for me is a move from within the Arnoldian tradition of English studies towards an understanding of culture and society through people like Raymond Williams, an understanding of the class nature of politics in Britain through someone like Edward Thompson, and an understanding of the importance of mass media and contemporary forms of life through people like Stuart Hall. My introduction to cultural studies was through politics within literary studies, during the 1960s and 1970s, and I think cultural studies still has a lot of that about it.

Cultural studies has abandoned some of that project now, as it's become more and more sociological over the years. It's interesting to me that the Birmingham Centre for Cultural Studies started out as part of the Department of English and it's now part of the Department of Sociology. I think that's a very significant move, and it's one that I regret. So I understand that cultural studies had to emancipate itself from the dead hand of literary departments, but at the same time it didn't necessarily have to abandon a lot of the interests in textual matters, aesthetic matters, the sense of living a culture rather than just living in a culture.

WB: *If you had to offer a brief description of cultural studies as it currently stands, say to a student taking up the subject, how would you sum it up in a few sentences?*

JH: Well, cultural studies has started to name itself quite easily these days. It's the study of power within the context of meaning. So if you're looking at the contemporary media, for example, cultural studies is classically the way in which media meanings reproduce relations of power, usually unequal relations of power, based on class or some other kind of demographic difference. That's the standard approach to cultural studies, these days. Power and meaning.

WB: *Would you recommend it as a subject, to a student?*

JH: I would recommend students to find out as much as they can about the world, and then try and understand why cultural studies is important. My own interest in cultural studies was formed at the postgraduate level, and it was in reaction to quite a lot of the things I'd done as an undergraduate. However, I think it's very important, I don't think it has thought itself through the problems it set itself twenty years ago yet, and I think undergraduates would understand more about the world through that particular explanatory framework. So I'm still a fan of it.

Popular Reality (1996)

WB: *How is a book like* Popular Reality *actually created? Can you talk me through the process from your first ideas to the writing of the manuscript?*

JH: In this particular context, *Popular Reality* was a departure for me. It was a book about journalism, and I wasn't aware of any other book on journalism which had been done from a cultural studies perspective. So that was the project of it, to study journalism from that point of view. And also, at this particular time in my career, I thought it was very important to move away from the endless present tense of textual analysis in the here and now, and to actually start writing some history. So I wanted to understand, and I wanted people to understand, how journalism had grown up as a textual institution, and what its history was. And at that time it so happened that there was a lot of discussion, in the journals and new books that came out, about modernity. It was when modernity was having its big revival, just a little bit after postmodernity. So it was kind of a gift. I wanted to talk about journalism, about cultural studies, I wanted to do it from a historical perspective. And then there was the question of modernity. It wrote itself. It was easy after that.

WB: *So you spent a long period preparing, and then wrote the actual manuscript in a short time.*

JH: Yes, I suppose that's why I laid out those elements beforehand. The writing was very quick, because I spent a long time preparing for it. The ideas were forming and cooking, as it were, a long time before I started writing it down, and what made it possible to write it very quickly was having this idea about the beginnings of political modernity, and taking those notions into particular forms of journalism.

WB: *And the visual texts which you incorporate so liberally ... were they building up over a long period of time, and simply fitted in?*

JH: Very much so. That's what happens to me all the time. In fact it's like a bit of an obsession, because it doesn't stop. So I'm still interested in some of the themes in that book, and I'm still collecting. There are things from *Picture Post* I've never given up on. Perhaps I'm less interested in Kylie than I used to be, but not in issues of what she represents for me. So I have a running habit of just browsing magazines and newspapers, TV shows and the rest of it, and selecting stuff which might be useful.

WB: *Do you have a running archive?*

JH: Yes, absolutely. That's what I do, but it's not a systematic one, it's very loose. It's basically junk on shelves, until such time as something comes up. But I do the same with academic books as well. Sometimes a book can be on the shelf for ten or fifteen years, and you suddenly realise: it fits here. So that's how I work. I amass materials, and then they make sense quite quickly at a given point.

WB: *How would you reply to the criticism that* Popular Reality, *perhaps like cultural studies itself, is concerned with trivia and ephemerality, with trash culture such as tabloids, breakfast cereals and pop stars?*

JH: Well, of course people are entitled to their point of view. What I'm trying to point out is that there are forms of politics arising from trash culture that ought to be taken more seriously. In this case it is that the notions of the public sphere and political culture are very masculine, very exclusive and don't take account of a great many aspects of people's lives. So if you're interested in ordinary life and what I call 'an anthropology of the everyday', most social theory of power just misses it. I'm interested in what goes on outside of all that. I always have been. That's really what motivates me. The point of view of the viewer, and the audience, and just the ordinary chap.

WB: *The ordinary girl, perhaps, as well.*

JH: Yes, I'm interested in them too ... well, I know a bit more about them now I've got daughters. But you know, the bluff ordinary chap, and his buffeting by cruel fate. That sort of stuff. And that's where trivia, trash and so on exists. What's it for? How is it used? Is it responding to any actual needs and functions in people's lives? And I think the answer is yes. I think it's demonstrably yes. So, first of all take it seriously, and then try and account for it. And what *Popular Reality* does, to my entire satisfaction, is write a history of journalism which says this stuff has always been around, since the beginning of modernity anyway, and it's political. So journalism as a textual system has these postmodern, trivial, trashy aspects, but when you look at these things it turns out they have quite strong political consequences. Politics is moving towards culture and identity, and that's where this kind of journalism blazed the trail. It was there first.

WB: *More fundamentally, some academics within cultural studies itself would argue with your exclusive focus on textual analysis, rather than, say, ethnography, a study of ownership and technology, or a socio-historical perspective. Can you enlarge on this dispute within cultural studies and briefly justify your own approach?*

JH: Okay, there are such disputes, no doubt about it. I don't have a dispute with anthropology. I don't like certain kinds of audience ethnography because I think they're banal, and answer foregone conclusions. When you have a social science or a social theory approach to culture, and you say, of course culture is a result of structural patterns in society, or economic ownership and control of organisations or whatever, and therefore you must talk about these and not about everyday lives of ordinary people, I just say, well, there's lots of people doing that. You know, you can read those books over there. I'm not saying that these things are not true. What I am saying is that there is a point of view of the audience, there is a consumption side of things, it does behove us to try and understand it, and that's what I do. Other people with their specialisms can do what they want to do. So I think that the mutual suspicion and name-calling is much more to do with institutional elbowing for resources, and not to do with trying to understand the object of study.

Hartley

WB: *Many of the key figures in cultural studies' history seem to have come from 'outside' in terms of their own personal background – I'm thinking of Hoggart's working-class childhood in Leeds, Williams coming* *to Cambridge from Abergavenny, and Hall from Jamaica to Oxford. Cultural studies seems to have been written largely by what Matthew Arnold called 'aliens', and your own personal background, as suggested by the passage about your absent father in* The Politics of Pictures, *seems also to fit this pattern. What are your feelings about the role of the 'outsider' in cultural studies?*

JH: I think there's a lot of truth in that, and it is actually a social movement. I mean, we're now talking about a period after the Second World War when there was what was called at the time an 'influx' – the same word that was used for Asians, and aliens of other kinds – of non-standard graduates into the universities. This was the era when the universities started opening up, and I'm very much part of that generation. I'm the first member of my family to go to university. I also had a very peculiar childhood. I went to an orphanage, and my family was relatively cut off from other contacts in various ways, so yes, I've always felt that I'm an observer of things going on that I'm trying to understand, rather than a direct participant. My own definition of this is 'not-quiteness'. It's like you're there, and you understand, and you're interested, and you're part of what's going on, but you're just tilted a bit. You're not quite the mainstream player. I think this is also where British comedy comes from. People who've had non-standard, or strange, or weird, or damaged childhoods often make good observers, whether they take the academic direction like I have or possibly the comedy direction like all the Monty Python people, right up to Stephen Fry. They've all got some peculiarity that they're having to deal with. I don't have ambitions to run the society that I'm interested in. You know, I wouldn't know what to do if I were made a banker or something. What really intrigues me, what arouses my curiosity, is how everything works. So I think it's necessary to have a stance from slightly outside it, but nevertheless to be fully engaged with it.

Cultural Studies: futures

WB: *Since your appointment at Cardiff you have established the Tom Hopkinson Centre for Media Research, which takes on PhD students from around the world, and launched the International Journal of Cultural Studies. How do these two projects reflect the way you see cultural studies developing towards and beyond the millennium?*

JH: There's one obvious thing that they do share, and that is that I'm very keen on making cultural studies international, because it already is. But there's a habit in Britain, particularly, and also in America, of thinking: well, we invented it so we don't have to think about it. You know, and others have to think about what we think. Well, they don't. There is very interesting work on culture, on meaning, on the relations between identity, power and everyday life, going on elsewhere. So I'm very interested in the international aspect of cultural studies from that point of view, of us learning from other academic and intellectual traditions about the study of culture.

I'm also interested in the international exchange of culture. Everybody talks about globalisation, and it's not entirely spurious. There is a lot of internationalisation going on of cultural productions in the form of movies and computer products. There's much more personal mobility than there used to be. People travel around more than they used to, so that even poor students can have, say, a summer in very far-flung places which they would never have thought of in my day. So there's a lot more international mobility, and I really am interested in that. I have a travel bug, so I like to go to places and see what's going on. I have that curiosity. So that's something I'd like to see cultural studies doing, concentrating on the international aspect both of academic life and of the object of study.

The other thing I'd like to see cultural studies doing is thinking carefully about very large-scale social changes, in the way that it always has had the ambition to do. Being something like the philosophical or social theory of our times. Because the way capitalist development and social and governmental development are going is towards some kind of integration between the old separate functions of government, education and media, and the old separate industries of, say, advertising, journalism and public relations. They're all integrating, they're all becoming much more like each other. And it behoves people thinking about the production and exchange of meaning to try and predict, try and understand what is going on there. This integration or convergence between discipline, pleasure and citizenship strikes me as being very much in need of explanation, and cultural studies has some well-honed tools to do that sort of work.

WB: *You've had strong links with Australian cultural studies. Do you see this as one of the new directions for cultural studies, which after all started in Britain, moved through Europe to America …*

JH: Well, that's an interesting point. Oddly enough I don't think Europe, certainly not Francophone Europe, has done cultural studies in the way that it's done in Britain. In fact they probably wouldn't even recognise it. So I don't think it's a European phenomenon.

WB: *I was thinking of Bourdieu, de Certeau ...*

JH: Well, that's true, but Bourdieu would call himself a sociologist, I think. He's got reasons for wanting to stick to that disciplinary label. Major work, obviously, and of interest to us, but I'm not sure it would be immediately recognisable as cultural studies. However, I think the straightforward tradition of British cultural studies has taken root elsewhere, particularly in North America and in Australia. In English-speaking developed countries, in other words. And as there are more English-speaking countries, for example Singapore, then cultural studies gains further interest. But I think it gains further interest because it has explanatory power. The thing about Australia, just to concentrate on that, is that Australia is not an imperial power in itself. It's a very strange country because it's a colony and yet made of settlers who themselves colonised the indigenous population.

WB: *It's got that sense of not-quiteness itself.*

JH: Yes, very much so. And cultural studies has been a very powerful tool of explanation of those kinds of things to do with identity, and the relation of Australian people to their national identity, their personal identity, their identity within the region. Which is odd. You know, they're a kind of white-trash nation marooned out to the east of Asia. There's lots to think about, and cultural studies has clearly proved useful in doing this. Australians are more self-conscious about their identity, citizenship and their cultural heritage than perhaps the English are. So cultural studies, there's no doubt, has more active participants, is more an active discourse, and is less demeaned by the organs of public enlightenment in Australia than it is in Britain.

WB: *How do you see the future of cultural studies? Will it become institutionalised and perhaps be accepted as a 'traditional' discipline; and would this absorption into the establishment effectively signal its end? Must cultural studies retain an element of radicalism and the spirit of the outsider, and can it do so?*

JH: I think cultural studies has already attained a certain amount of institutional respectability, and where it does it tends to fall flat on its face, actually. I do think it's more of a critical, questioning, quizzical, not-quite discourse than it is a magisterial one, so that if you teach cultural studies as a straightforward discipline, what is lost is the thing that made me do it in the first place. I needed it to explain the magisterial and mainstream discipline that I'd just studied. So I have my doubts about it being easily translated into a mainstream discipline. When it is translated into a mainstream discipline, it must necessarily become something else.

The other thing is that cultural studies is already breaking up, and where it is institutionalised it's quite clear that it is being set up by people who are not setting up departments of cultural studies and drawing in interdisciplinary forces with them. They are putting cultural studies on in existing departments of social science or in the literary area. So there is already a bit of fragmentation in the field, and although that's a shame I think it's inevitable. But it shows for certain that cultural studies has not achieved this status of being a single discipline. And it's interesting also that it's still hard to name. I've 'done' cultural studies since the early 1980s, late 1970s even, but I've never actually had cultural studies in my job description. I've always been either a lecturer or professor of communication, or mass communication, or media. So it's like semiotics, it's a method or a set of tools, but it's still not a subject in its own right.

Further reading

Hartley's oeuvre proper begins with *Reading Television*, his collaboration with John Fiske (Methuen, 1979), and is developed in the solo work *Understanding News* (Methuen, 1982). However, the mode I have called 'Hartleyism' – the daring historical leaps, the theoretical three-card montes and the inability to resist a pun – really kicks in with *Tele-ology* (Routledge, 1992), which emerged from Hartley's PhD thesis and goes into turbo with *The Politics of Pictures* (Routledge, 1992) and *Popular Reality* (Routledge, 1996). *Uses of Television* is scheduled for 1999.

8 | WHERE NEXT?

Outro

Where next? By which I mean, where next for cultural studies, and where next for you, the reader? Of course, there are many answers to both questions, and I hope that previous chapters have begun to supply them. Depending on what took your fancy, you may feel inclined to follow up the bibliography for Hoggart, or the further reading for Hall, and so begin your own line of detection along the roots of the subject's heritage which seem most promising. I have given just a sense of Cultural Studies' history and, by using my guidelines as you see fit, you can continue the research yourself, whether you choose to dig deeper or to branch outwards.

As for its futures, the last chapter offered John Hartley's vision of the discipline's potential fragmentation across academic departments and of its current trend, for good or ill, towards sociology rather than textual analysis. Hartley foresaw two alternative timelines, the first involving cultural studies' possible shift into the mainstream, 'magisterial' position which could rob it of all its power and appeal, and the second, witnessing the discipline's transformation into a new kind of philosophy for the twenty-first century.

These, of course, are the tentative prophecies of just one person, and it should be remembered that there are as many different sets of hopes and fears for the subject as there are academics working within it. Henry Jenkins, for instance, shared with me via e-mail his personal optimism for the discipline's future, which he sees as grounded in new technologies, such as that which enabled our own discussion, in fresh national perspectives from Canada and New Zealand, as well as from America and the UK, and in the younger generation of cultural theorists whose work, in his eyes, embodies a shift from high theory towards a closer engagement with popular texts, a move towards a more accessible, popular writing style and a broadening of cultural studies' readership in order to reach a genuinely popular audience. Jenkins' edited anthology *Hop On Pop* opens with a manifesto for this new generation of cultural studies; the wit and verve of its attempt to seize what it views as a transitional moment for the subject is suggested by the book's original title, *The BIG Duke Book of Fun*.

Meanwhile, I offer one of my own suggestions, which is glib, neat and incomplete but which has the advantage of serving both my initial questions at once. The suggestion is threefold, and can be summed up in one word.

Virtual ethnography: cultural studies about the internet

Cultural studies has spread itself through a process of island-hopping which recently landed it in Australia, Singapore, New Zealand, Canada and Hong Kong, among other locations. But it has also leapt sideways, through the looking-glass of the PC monitor, and begun to colonise the virtual nation-states of the World Wide Web. Books like *Virtual Culture* and *Internet Culture* are testament to this pioneer spirit; already the genre is beginning to subdivide and specialise as cultural studies' concern with the ambivalent and amorphous natures of sexual, ethnic and gendered identity on the Web leads it into ethnographic research of individuals' behaviour in virtual 'communities' such as chatrooms and newsgroups. Hopes for more egalitarian, even utopian virtual spaces where signs of gender and race shift or become irrelevant are tempered in these investigations by issues of, on one level, limited access to internet technology for some members of society and, on another, of abuse, racist 'flaming' or even 'virtual rape'.

This kind of cultural studies 'about' the internet is, by now, nothing new. Henry Jenkins' study of online audience response to *Twin Peaks* was published in 1994, to be followed by, among others, Susan J. Clerc's 1996 article on *X-Files* internet fandom and Roberta Pearson's similar project of 1997 on 'Sherlock Holmes in Cyberspace'. More generally, Steven G. Jones' *Virtual Culture*, David Porter's *Internet Culture* and Rob Shields' *Cultures of Internet* explore issues of online 'society', while feminist and queer theory have staked their claim in cyberspace through Dale Spender's *Nattering on the Net* and Nina Wakeford's 'Cyberqueer'.

In many ways of course this was inevitable, an act of *amor fati*; a discipline thriving on the diverse, the radical, the popular and the modern discovers a near-infinite archive of subcultures, fangroups, trivia and home-made artifacts, updated by the second and begging to be colonised. Yet the contemporary project to translate the web into print, with authors playing tourist-guide for armchair travellers who don't even have to own a PC to sample the internet's exoticism, can also read as a process of containment, flattening and making safe; on one level it seems perversely inappropriate, like trying to fit a 3D image into a two-dimensional frame. One of the net's primary characteristics is its interactivity; the mode of reading it requires a leap-frogging, improvisational act from link to link, jump to jump, which in turn inscribes its own trail on the web. Looking back where you came, you may wonder how you got from a railway timetable through an All Saints gallery and the Sprite website to an article on Michel Foucault and *Twelve Monkeys*, but you're glad you did. Rather than the way-dude west-Coastism of 'surfing', the process should perhaps be called 'wandering', in the sense intended by the Situationists and Michel de Certeau; if taking your own route through the net is 'walking in the city', reading a book on internet culture can never be much more than studying a map.

Building sites: cultural studies on the internet

There is a fundamental logic, then, behind cultural studies websites; their analysis and debate are 'on' the web, but they are also 'of' it, immersed in its unruliness, only ever one jump away from a Barbie fanpage or an advertisement for propane accessories. They are in a unique position to react to and with their surroundings instantly, to invite debate from every reader who drops by an incorporate responses into the text, so developing a far more organic, less rigid form of academic study than would ever be possible in a quarterly journal or even a fanzine. At its least imaginative, on-line cultural studies constitutes little more than an advertisement for the print version, and wastes the medium to do a job more appropriate to a mailshot. The sites discussed below all transcend that level at least, though they have their moments of clumsiness and their flaws. Some are on-line journals, some merely collections of links; both are in the process of finding themselves, as the 'Under Construction' signs on many pages readily indicate. At their best, though, these sites are thrilling not so much for their content but for what they wring from that unique form, for their recognition that reading, here more than anywhere, is an act of participation, and for the possibilities which that recognition brings. In their dynamic nature and their openness to change, online journals are in a position to question what cultural studies could mean, perhaps should mean; through the very diversity of their contents they suggest a number of answers and point to a variety of possible futures for the discipline.

For this reason alone, I would recommend the following sites as a perfect answer to that 'where next', in terms of your own next step. Not only will they give you a vivid picture of cultural studies as it currently stands – coming far closer to the state of the art than I could ever hope to here – they also provide archives of incredible diversity and depth. Projects like the on-line journal *Bad Subjects* or the resource centre *Voice of the Shuttle* provide reams of regularly-updated articles on contemporary issues, alongside classic texts by familiar names like Adorno; while sometimes baffling, these juxtapositions may prompt you to join up dots, take unexpected detours, to follow that maxim 'only connect'. With just a few links and jumps you can take your investigations to intriguing conclusions. If the eight fan-sites on Michel Foucault offered by *Voice of the Shuttle* don't float your boat, there's always the link, though *Cult Stud-L*, to John Fiske's homepage; and if you don't like either of those avenues, there are multiple possibilities for you to post up your own opinions, take part in discussion threads and add your own voice to the debates of virtual cultural studies.

This, inevitably, will be itself just another map, its finer details out of date as soon as it sees print: but the addresses are there, and I can only urge you to visit the city.

Bad Subjects

One of the net's most significant assets is its interactivity. Another, surely, is the sense of community it offers, and the Bad Subjects Collective is the closest cultural studies gets to an on-line fan-club. If spawning the term 'badsubjectian' to describe its dissident, irreverent brand of cult-studs wasn't enough, the sheer number of its articles circulating in other journals is testament to its influence. The current issue to date, devoted to 'Men, Women and Everyone Else', is typical of the journal's strengths and its minor weaknesses. While the twelve articles on offer are always witty and vibrant, they might also be seen as slightly disparate, a selection box of assorted musings rather than a concerted attempt to grasp the vast and slippery subjects the group sets itself. Undoubtedly, the sharp little pieces of *Bad Subjects* #38 and its successors will themselves remain on the net indefinitely, which itself tells us something about the shelf life of texts in this supposedly ephemeral medium; traditionalists will also be encouraged by the editors' quaint advice to 'print a perfect copy of our print edition and pass it on to friends'.

Cult Stud-L

The community spirit continues at this listings site which mutated from a resource for a University of South Florida postgraduate seminar to an international network of subscribers. Despite the selection of articles available, the site has more the air of a support network than a journal; hence the link for 'Job Openings' – which when I tried it apologised that none were currently on offer – and the opportunity to visit John Fiske's homepage or find out what fellow academics have been reading over the summer. As an invaluable bonus, CULTSTUD-L includes a FAQ – Frequently Asked Questions – which swiftly and thoroughly interrogates definitions of cultural studies, outlining its roots, politics and methods in the space of two pages with a rigour and economy I can only envy.

Sarah Zupko's Cultural Studies Center

A jolly-looking site after the utilitarian design of CULTSTUD-L, peppered with nifty little icons – 'Film' gets a clapperboard, 'Cyberspace/Sci-Fi' a flying saucer and 'Links', cutely, a section of chain. Following up those leads, however, begins to raise doubts about this system of categorisation. While diversity is one of the joys of both the net and cultural studies itself, it might be asked, when reams of *Dialectic of Enlightenment* appear next to a jokey piece on mall culture, whether there is a limit beyond which diversity risks edging into anarchy and the coherence of this type of site is threatened, with the sense that any distinction between new work and archive material is too easily being eroded. These are by no means faults of Zupko's site alone, yet this Center, by gathering common problems with on-line cultural studies into one place, begs significant and necessary questions.

Voice of the Shuttle: Cultural Studies Page

After the journal and the support network comes the archive. Above all this is an incredible resource, a vast file of information which although diverse is also methodically arranged and filed – here, for instance, Adorno is very properly under 'Frankfurt School', although fans of shopping malls can sate themselves with the three links to 'The Eighties'. The almost obsessive rigour and detail about this site, reflected in its chosen decor of intricate weaves, enables rich variety yet holds it in check, and ultimately gives an inspiringly inclusive sense of cultural studies with depth as well as breadth. If you ever wanted the choice of eight different homepages on Michel Foucault, this is your heaven.

The English Server: Cultural Studies and Critical Theory

Once past the opening menu which lists 'Cultural Theory' rather perversely, or perhaps tellingly, among 'Music', 'Fiction' and 'Recipes', this site like many others offers a brief definition of its subject, identifying the roots of cultural studies as sociology, gender studies, literary criticism and psychoanalysis. And again, as is the case with so many other sites, its full menu of available articles interrogates this definition, asking and providing a provisional answer to the question 'what is cultural studies?' In this case, the answer is a characteristic eclecticism, from a Jameson bibliography through an article by Adorno and another, adjacent, signed 'Anonymous', to the ubiquitous *Bad Subjects* offerings on Milli Vanili and Madonna. As with Sarah Zupko's page above, this variety-pack mentality can be frustrating, particularly when some links dead-end in the response 'Not Found'. Above all, though, this site reminds us of cultural studies' inherent potential for kitsch: where else, under a fancy calligraphic title and pretty logo of a country cottage, would you find the words 'Antonio Gramsci; followed by the bright yellow flash 'NEW!' like a label in a cut-price supermarket?

Cultural Studies Central

Idiosyncratic and witty from its title onwards, *Cultural Studies Central* opens with epigrams from Goering and Presley, and presents a definition of its subject as 'a simmering stew of the ideas, voices and lives of people all over the world. It's the things we use and the people we talk about. It's life and life only.' Well, that's alright, Ma ... but if this slightly loopy statement of intent risks deterring the more serious academic, the site's use of its chosen medium cannot be faulted. The stress is on interactivity, with a user-friendly database of urban legends to search, a 'rants and raves' bulletin board with on-going debates open to participation, and the promise of a 'multimedia bricolage of images, sounds and words' coming soon, with an invitation to contribute. Robin Markowitz's 'Reconstructing Michael Jackson' epitomises the site's project; a close analysis of various aspects of the Jackson phenomenon, it actively requests responses and builds them into the piece itself, resulting in a multi-authored string of contributions tied to the original object, whether the 'Billy Jean' video or Jackson's single 'white glove'. Embracing a tradition of visual history from the Mona Lisa to mid-Eighties pop video, *Cultural Studies Central* also takes the bravest steps of all the sites listed here towards visualising the way cultural studies debates could look at the start of the next millennium.

Home pages: cultural studies through the internet

Through the internet: that is, using the medium for its potential as a tool of instant and economical long-distance communication and information relay. At its most accessible – and here again is something you can try for yourself at home, at college, in a library, or cafe – the internet transports you right inside departments of cultural studies at universities around the country, with *carte blanche* to look at CVs, browse the faculty's latest articles, view upcoming or recent conference proceedings and even apply for courses by e-mail.

As an obvious destination, look to the University of Birmingham, England, which as Hartley points out currently houses the Department of Cultural Studies and Sociology. The list of staff profiles alone provides a neat sketch of the ways in which cultural studies is currently being constructed at this most influential of academic centres: one professor editing a collection on world perspectives of cultural studies, another publishing in both English and Spanish, while a third lecturer works on 'racisms, sexualities, cultural geographies, fun, excitement and showing off'.

The department's most recent conference to date, on 'Mixed Race' from a mainly sociological angle, and the number of postgraduate researchers engaged with 'gay urban spaces', suggest that issues of ethnicity and sexuality are still yielding valuable debate and prompting new avenues of exploration. The evidence here implies that this variation on established themes is being enabled through a hybridisation of previously distinct areas ('illness and sexual identity'), a subdivision into more specific zones ('South-Asian British female identity') or a cross-pollination with other approaches ('Hong Kong, feminism, cultural imperialism and Star TV').

As with the Tom Hopkinson Centre at the University of Cardiff, there is a cheering sense of heritage here and a tip of the hat to the past; as is so often the case on the internet, history concertinas so that the ancient 'stencilled papers' from the CCCS are advertised next to the latest issue of the department's new journal. It seems sweetly fitting that spankingly recent articles on 'Birmingham and the New European Reconstruction' and 'McDonald's in Moscow', by the department's newest talents, appear alongside Dick Hebdige on Mods from 1971, Stuart Hall on Marx from 1973 and Angela McRobbie on *Jackie* from 1978. Cultural studies, at Birmingham as elsewhere, often has one eye on the future and the other, fondly, nostalgically and respectfully, on the route it took to get this far.

Anecdotes

I visited Birmingham itself late last year (1997), to give a conference paper – on gay readings of Batman comics in the 1950s – and I insisted that I be shown the tower, now in disrepair but under reconstruction, where the CCCS used to meet; it felt, even now, like a mecca. Later that week I was fortunate enough to meet Richard Hoggart, himself giving a paper at the University of Wales. If Birmingham was a site of pilgrimage, here was a prophet: white-haired and canny, crouched over a cane marked 'HOGGART' and talking rather like one of those housewives he described in 1920s Leeds, with just the right measure of self-mockery to save him from dogmatism.

He spoke of the conveyor-belt mentality of current Cultural Studies publishing, with its trends and buzz-words and 'waffle-iron' templates of fashionable ideas which every new writer felt bound to follow: and he spoke of the young Simon Hoggart – now a journalist – banging on the sides of the metal shed where his father, cocooned with an electric fire, was writing *The Uses of Literacy* before dinner. And he spoke, surrounded now by a host of staff and research students, of the community where he now lives and of the shopkeeper who greeted him with 'You're the one wrote that book about us ... it was good, I read it.'

Hoggart crinkled his eyes and sipped at his glass of sherry; and I intended to ask what it meant to him that he could still command such an appreciative academic crowd with his opinions on the future of cultural studies, and at the same time touch and please the 'ordinary' people who had been his concern for over forty years, but a naivety took me and I asked instead 'Are you glad? Does that make you glad?'

'Appen it does,' said Hoggart. 'Appen it does.'

FURTHER READING

Susan J. Clerc, "DDEB, GATB, MPPB and Ratboy: The X-Files' Media Fandom, Online and Off," in David Lavery, Angela Hague, Marla Cartwright (eds.), *Deny All Knowledge: Reading the X-Files*, London, Faber and Faber (1996)

Helen Fallon, *WOW: Women on the Web*, University College Dublin (1997)

Richard Hoggart, *The Way We Live Now*, Pimlico (1996)

Henry Jenkins, "Do You Enjoy Making The Rest Of Us Feel Stupid? alt.tv.twinpeaks, the Trickster Author and Viewer Mastery", in David Lavery (ed.) *Full of Secrets: Critical Approaches to Twin Peaks*, Detroit: Wayne State University Press (1994)

Henry Jenkins, Tara McPherson, Jane Shattuc (eds.) *Hop On Pop: The Politics and Pleasures of Popular Culture*, Duke University Press (forthcoming 1999)

Steven G. Jones, *Virtual Culture*, Sage (1997)

Roberta Pearson, "It's Always 1985: Sherlock Holmes in Cyberspace", in Deborah Cartmell, IQ Hunter, Heidi Kaye and Imelda Whelehan (eds.) *Trash Aesthetics*, London, Pluto Press (1997)

David Porter (ed.), *Internet Culture*, Routledge (1997)

Howard Rheingold, *The Virtual Community: Homesteading on the Electronic Frontier*, New York: Addison Wesley (1993)

Rob Shields (ed.) *Cultures of Internet*, Sage (1996)

Dale Spender, *Nattering on the Net: Women, Power and Cyberspace*, Spinifex Press (1995)

Nina Wakeford, "Cyberqueer", in Andy Medhurst and Sally Munt, *Lesbian and Gay Studies*, Cassell (1997)

USEFUL ADDRESSES

Bad Subjects, http://english-server.hss.cmu.edu/bs

Birmingham Department of Cultural Studies and Sociology, http://www.bham.ac.uk/CulturalStudies

Cultstud-L, http://www.cas.usf.edu/communication/rodman/cultstud/main.html

Culture and Communication Reading Room, http://kali.murdoch.edu.au/~cntinuum

Cultural Studies Central, http://home.earthlink.net/~rmarkowitz

CTheory, http://www.ctheory.com

The English Server, http://english-server.hss.cmu.edu

Media and Communications Site, http://www.aber.ac.uk/~dgc/media.html

Sarah Zupko's Cultural Studies Center, http://www.mcs.net/~zupko/popcult.htm.

Voice of the Shuttle: Cultural Studies, http://humanitas.ucsb.edu/shuttle/cultural.html

INDEX

active readership theory 100
Adorno, T.W. 12, 16–22, 134, 136
  on advertising 21–2, 56
  on art 19–20
  and Barthes 41
  and Berger 41, 56, 58
  on commodity fetishisation 18–19
  on the culture industry 17–18,
    19–20, 27, 28
  Dialectic of Enlightenment (Adorno
    and Horkheimer) 17, 19, 20
  further reading on 10–11, 21
  and Hoggart 24, 27, 28
  and Jenkins 116
  and Williams 21, 37, 39
advertising
  Adorno on 21–2, 56
  Berger on 54–6
  Leavis on 14–15
'aliens' 9–10, 127
anarchy 7, 8, 9
appropriation 65, 66
Arnold, Matthew 6–11, 127
  and Barthes 41
  and Berger 41
  Culture and Anarchy 6, 7–10, 15
  and Hebdige 64
  and Hoggart 24, 30–1
  and Leavis 13, 15
  poetry 11
  and Williams 10, 11, 33–4, 36, 40
art
  Adorno on 19–20
  Berger 51–2
  Hoggart on working-class 26–7
audiences
  Fiske on popular culture and 102–3,
    106–7

  history of 70
  Morley on television 71–5, 100, 113,
    115
  online 132
Australian cultural studies 123, 128, 129
avant-garde culture 16, 26, 41
Avengers, The 120

Bad Subjects (online journal) 134–5, 136
Bakhtin, Michel 107
Barbarians 9, 10
Barthes, Roland 41, 42–8
  and Fiske 102, 107
  and Hall 64
  and Hebdige 64–5, 69
  on myth 44–7
  Mythologies 41, 42–7, 58, 64, 67–8
  on semiology and language 43
Benjamin, Walter 16, 17, 19
  and Berger 58
  'The Work of Art in the Age of
    Mechanical Reproduction' 21, 52
Bentham, Jeremy 33, 86
Berger, John 16, 37, 41, 48–58, 81
  on art, mystification and ownership
    51–2
  and Hall 64
  novels 49, 57
  on publicity 54–6
  and the visual representation of
    women 53–4
  Ways of Seeing 22, 41, 49–56, 58, 94
Birmingham Centre for Contemporary
    Cultural Studies 23, 30–1, 60–4,
    69, 76, 82, 123
  and feminist research 80–1
  and Fiske 102, 103, 104
  on the Internet 137, 138

Bloom, Harold 1, 2
Bourdieu, Pierre 58, 89–94, 101, 129
    Certeau on 94, 95–6
    Distinction 48, 89–93
    and Fiske 102, 107
    on habitus 90–2, 93, 97
    and Jenkins 121
Bowie, David 66
Brabazon, Tara 123
bricolage 65, 98, 102
Brunsdon, Charlotte 75, 76, 80–1, 113

Cagney and Lacey 103
capital, economic and cultural 90, 91,
    93, 94
carceral society 86–7, 88
categorizing and labelling 67
CCCS *see* Birmingham Centre for
    Contemporary Cultural Studies
Centre for Contemporary Cultural
    Studies *see* Birmingham Centre
    for Contemporary Cultural Studies
Centre of European Sociology 89
Certeau, Michel de 87, 88, 93, 94–100,
    101, 111, 133
    and Fiske 102, 103, 104, 107
    and Jenkins 115, 117–18, 121
    and *la perruque* 97, 99, 100
    on strategies and tactics 96–7, 99–100
    The Practice of Everyday Life 95–7, 99
    on walking in the city 98
Change in the Village (Sturt) 14, 34
Christianity 8
city, walking in the 98
class differences, in mealtimes in
    France 92
Clerc, Susan J. 132
Coleridge, Samuel Taylor 6, 33
Collini, Stefan, *Arnold* 11
commodity fetishisation, and use value
    18–19
common culture 38–9
communication 36–7
Corrigan, Paul 62
Crossroads (television programme) 73, 75
Cult Stud-L 134, 135
cultural capital 90, 91

Cultural Studies Central 136–7
culture industry 17–18, 19–20, 27, 28
cyberpunk 100

Dissenters 7
Docker, John 20, 27, 30
Doing as one Likes 7, 8–9
dominant readings, of television
    messages 71, 72–3
During, Simon 24, 63

Eagleton, Terry 40
Eco, Umberto 107
election propaganda 70
Eliot, T.S. 15, 33, 67
ethnographic research 62–3, 78, 80, 126
exchange value 18

fan culture 113–20
feminist theory 80–1
    and the Birmingham CCCS 60, 62–3
    and the Internet 132
    and romance 108–13, 115
    and youth culture 75–81
fields of power 92–3
Fish, Stanley 75, 113
Fiske, John 64, 70, 75, 99, 100, 101–7, 111
    and Hartley 122, 130
    on the Internet 134
    and Jenkins 115, 116, 118, 121
    on Madonna 103, 106–7
    Reading the Popular 102–4, 107
    Understanding Popular Culture
    102, 116
folk culture 13, 15
Foucault, Michel 42, 48, 64, 67, 82,
    83–8, 101
    on the carceral society 86–7, 88
    Certeau on 87, 88, 95–6
    Discipline and Punish 83–8
    and Fiske 103, 107
    on the Internet 133, 134, 136
    on punishment as spectacle 83–5
    on surveillance and the panopticon
    85–6, 87–8, 95, 97
Frankfurt School 17, 70, 136
French theory 82–100, 101, 102

Fry, Stephen 127

Garber, Jennie 63
Genet, Jean 65, 67
Gibson, Mark 123
Gibson, William 100
Gilroy, Paul 69
girls, working-class teenage 76–80
good art 19
good bad art 19–20
Gramsci, Antonio 6, 136

Habermas, Jurgen 17
habitus 90–2, 93, 97
Hall, Stuart 11, 24, 30, 40, 48, 49, 82, 93,
        127, 131
    on the black 'mugger' 61, 88
    and the CCCS 59–60, 63
    and feminism 63
    and Fiske 102, 103, 107
    and Hartley 122, 123
    and Hebdige 65, 69
    and hegemony 61
    on the Internet 138
    and Jenkins 115, 121
    and Morley 71
    Policing the Crisis 61, 64
    and polysemy 61–2
Hals, Frans 51–2, 58
Hartley, John 4, 16, 58, 75, 107, 131
    and Hartleyism 122–3
    interview with 123–30
    The Politics of Pictures 122, 127, 130
    Popular Reality 122, 124–6, 130
Hebdige, Dick 11, 30, 62, 63, 64–9, 100
    and Fiske 102, 105
    further reading on 69
    on the Internet 138
    and McRobbie 75–6
    problems with 68–9
    and the punk movement 11, 65, 66,
        67, 68, 97
    Subculture 64–8, 69, 76
Hebraism 7, 8
hegemony 61, 66–7
Hellenism 7, 8, 13
high culture 13
Hobson, Dorothy 75, 113

Hoggart, Richard 14, 15–16, 21, 23–31,
        41, 126, 131
    and the CCCS 60, 138
    on current Cultural Studies 138–9
    and Fiske 102, 104
    and Hall 59, 60, 61–2, 64
    and Hartley 122
    and Hebdige 64, 68, 69
    and the oral tradition 25–6
    social background 24, 90, 91
    The Uses of Literacy 23, 24–9, 59, 60,
        62, 92, 102, 104
    and Williams 23–4, 39
Hoggart, Simon 30, 138
homosexuality 67, 118–19, 120–1
Horkheimer, Max 16, 17
Hulme, T.E. 33
Huxley, Aldous, *Brave New World* 35

incorporation 66–7
*International Journal of Cultural
        Studies* 122, 127
Internet 132–8
Internet Culture 132
interpretive communities, television
        audiences as 71, 72, 74

Jackie magazine 78–9, 138
Jackson, Michael 137
Jenkins, Henry 62, 69, 88, 99, 101, 104,
        107
    on the future of cultural studies 131–2
    on Hartley 122
    Hop on Pop 132
    and Radway 112, 113, 115
    and slash 118–19
    Textual Poachers 100, 107, 113–20
    'The Velveteen Rabbit' 102, 116
Johnson, Richard 60
Jones, Steven G. 132
journalism
    in *Culture and Environment* 12–13
    in Hartley's *Popular Reality* 124, 126
Joyce, James, *Ulysses* 15
Just Seventeen magazine 78–80, 81, 82

Kristeva, Julia 68–9

Lacan, Jacques 42
language, and semiology 43
Lawrence, D.H. 33
Le Pen, Jean-Marie 47
Leavis, F.R. 6, 11–16
    and Adorno 16, 21
    and Arnold 13, 15, 40
    and Barthes 41
    and Berger 41
    Culture and Environment (Levis and
        Thompson) 11, 12–13, 15, 16, 23,
        34, 37, 49, 57
    The Great Tradition 11–12, 13, 15
    and Hall 59
    on high culture 13
    and Hoggart's *The Uses of Literacy*
        24, 26, 27, 31
    on organic culture 14, 15, 25, 34
    and *Scrutiny* 12, 13, 15
    and Williams 15, 16, 33, 34, 37, 39, 40
Leavis, Q.D. 12, 15, 31, 40
Lévi-Strauss, Claude 42, 89
Liberalism 7, 8–9
lifestyle choices, and habitus 91–2
Lorrain, Jorge 60
Lumby, Catharine 123

McKee, Alan 123
McRobbie, Angela 63, 64, 81, 107, 108
    Feminism and Youth Culture 69,
        75–81, 113
    on the Internet 138
    Resistance Through Rituals 76
Madonna 103, 106–7, 136
male subcultures 75–7
Marcuse, Herbert 17
Markowitz, Robin 137
Marx Brothers 20
Marxism 12, 16, 64, 82
mass culture 14, 35–7
masses, people seen as 36
Merquior, J.G., *Foucault* 87–8
Merton, Robert 70
metalanguage, myth as a 44
micropolitics 99, 101, 104, 110, 115
Mill, John Stuart 33
Miller, Toby 120
Minogue, Kylie 123, 125

'mob', fears of the 11, 36
mods 65, 66
Moriarty, Michael 47
Morley, David 63, 100
    and Fiske 102
    and Jenkins 115, 119, 121
    The *'Nationwide' Audience* 62, 70–5,
        80, 113
'muggers' 61, 67, 88
music 67, 68
mystification 51–2
myth 44–7

naked women, in paintings 53–4
Nationwide audience study 62, 70–5,
    80, 82
Nazi Germany, Adorno and 20–1, 56
negotiated readings, of television
        messages 71, 73–4
negotiation 66
newspapers 12–13, 36
novels 36

oppositional readings, of television
        messages 71, 73
oral tradition 25–6
O'Regan, Tom 123
organic culture 14, 15, 25, 34
Orwell, George 30, 33, 39, 40
    Nineteen EightyFour 35, 87
outsider, the 67–8

panopticon, surveillance and the 85–6,
        87–8, 95, 97
Pearson, Roberta 132
Philistines 9, 10
Picture Post 122, 125
politicised speech, myth as 44–6
polysemy 61–2, 71
Populace, in Arnold's *Culture and
        Anarchy* 9, 10
Porter, David 132
propaganda 70
publicity, Berger on 54–6
punishment, as spectacle 83–5
punk movement 11, 65, 66, 67, 68, 69, 97
Puritanism 7, 8

queer reading 120–1

Radway, Janice 62, 99, 100, 104
    Jenkins on 112, 113, 115, 119, 121
    Reading the Romance 81, 108–13
rap music 67
Reagan, Ronald 104, 105
romance, and feminism 108–13, 115

Saussure, Ferdinand de 42–3, 48
science fiction fans 69
Scrutiny (literary journal) 12, 13, 15
semiology
    Hebdige on 64–5
    and language 43
    in McRobbie's analysis 78–9, 80
Shaw, George Bernard 33
Shields, Rob 132
slash fiction 118–19, 120
stagnation, Williams on 37
Star Trek 113–14, 116, 117, 118
Star-Dust in Hollywood 14, 34
strategies and tactics 96–7, 99–100
Strinati, Dominic 20
structures of feeling 34, 35
Sturt, George 14, 34
subcultures
    male 75–7
    see also youth culture
surveillance, and the panopticon 85–6,
    87–8, 95, 97

teds 65, 66
television audiences
    Jenkins on fans 113–20
    Morley on 71–5, 100
Thatcher, Margaret 38, 105
Thompson, Denys 11, 12, 15, 49
Thompson, Edward 123
Turner, Graeme 74, 123

United States of America 101
use value, and commodity fetishisation
    18–19
'uses and gratifications' theory 70, 71

Vicious, Sid 67
video games 104–5
Virtual Culture 132
Voice of the Shuttle 134, 136

Wark, McKenzie 123
Wheelwright's Shop, The (Sturt) 14, 34
Williams, Raymond 31–40, 126–7
    and Adorno 21, 39
    and Arnold 10, 11, 33–4, 40
    and Barthes 41
    and Berger 41, 51
    and common culture 38–9
    Culture and Society 3, 23, 31, 32–3,
        38, 40, 59
    and Hall 59, 60, 64
    and Hartley 122, 123
    and Hebdige 64, 69
    and Hoggart 23–4, 30
    and Leavis 15, 16, 33, 34, 37, 39
    The Long Revolution 31, 32, 33, 38–9
    and mass culture 35–7
    and Oxbridge 93
    and stagnation 37
    and structures of feeling 34, 35
Willis, Paul 31, 69, 113
    and Fiske 105, 107
    Learning to Labour 69, 76, 78
    and McRobbie 75, 76
Winship, Janice 63, 81
women, Berger and the visual
    representation of 53–4
working-class culture 24–9

youth culture
    feminism and 75–81
    and Madonna 106–7
    punk movement 11, 65, 66, 67, 68,
        69, 97
    and video games 104–5
    Willis on 31, 69, 76, 78, 105

Zupko, Sarah, Cultural Studies Center
    135, 136

ty TEACH YOURSELF

FILM STUDIES

Warren Buckland

Teach Yourself Film Studies provides a clear and concise introduction to the exciting world of film. The book offers an overview of the key areas in film studies, including:

- aesthetics – covering the artistic nature of film and its different techniques
- narrative – including narrative logic and the different types of narration
- genres – with emphasis on melodrama, *film noir* and 1950s science fiction film
- documentary films – covering the different formats adopted over the history of film making.

Throughout, the reader will find detailed discussions of the films of important directors, ranging from Orson Welles and Alfred Hitchcock, Jean-Luc Godard and Wim Wenders, to Martin Scorsese, Quentin Tarantino, Mike Leigh and John Dahl.

The book ends by uncovering the secrets of film reviewing – the conventions reviewers adopt when they write about and evaluate films.

Whatever your interest in film, this book will provide the necessary information and critical skills to turn you into a well-informed film critic.

Warren Buckland is a Lecturer in Screen Studies at Liverpool John Moores University, and writes on film theory, criticism and contemporary Hollywood cinema.

POSTMODERNISM

Glenn Ward

One of the most fiercely disputed terms of the late twentieth century, postmodernism has had an impact in most fields, from literature and the visual arts, to cultural studies and sociology. In each of these areas, the meanings of postmodernism are flexible, but in all cases it forces us to question some of our most cherished assumptions. Postmodern debates suggest that our most ingrained ideas about the nature of history, culture, meaning and identity can no longer be taken for granted. As such, it has far-reaching implications for how we think about the world today.

This book is an indispensable guide to this sometimes demanding terrain. Aimed at readers encountering theories of postmodernism for the first time, it places the subject in a wide context. Rather than give an account of the 'postmodern condition' from a single perspective, it offers an introduction to the most important theorists in a number of different disciplines, and links theoretical questions to an eclectic range of examples, from both 'high' and 'popular' culture.

Glenn Ward is a lecturer in the Faculty of Art and Music at Bath College of Art and Design.

Other related titles

TEACH YOURSELF

MEDIA STUDIES

Brenda Downes and Steve Miller

What is Media Studies? Why has it become the fastest growing subject area in post-16 education? How can our own experience and knowledge of the media help us when studying them?

The book provides a clear introduction for those embarking on a course of study and for those who wish to have an overview of current debates about the media.

Teach Yourself Media Studies

- explains concepts used in Media Studies
- introduces essential knowledge for 16+ examinations
- discusses issues central to the study of the media
- uses examples across a range of media technologies
- suggests relevant practical activities
- offers a guide to further study.

The authors have a wide experience of teaching media through all age ranges up to and including graduate and post-graduate level, and are currently producing educational material in a variety of media.